Digital Libraries:
Integrating Content and Systems

CHANDOS
INFORMATION PROFESSIONAL SERIES

Series Editor: Ruth Rikowski
(email: Rikowskigr@aol.com)

Chandos' new series of books are aimed at the busy information professional. They have been specially commissioned to provide the reader with an authoritative view of current thinking. They are designed to provide easy-to-read and (most importantly) practical coverage of topics that are of interest to librarians and other information professionals. If you would like a full listing of current and forthcoming titles, please visit our web site **www.chandospublishing.com** or contact Hannah Grace-Williams on email info@chandospublishing.com or telephone number +44 (0) 1865 884447.

New authors: we are always pleased to receive ideas for new titles; if you would like to write a book for Chandos, please contact Dr Glyn Jones on email gjones@chandospublishing.com or telephone number +44 (0) 1865 884447.

Bulk orders: some organisations buy a number of copies of our books. If you are interested in doing this, we would be pleased to discuss a discount. Please contact Hannah Grace-Williams on email info@chandospublishing.com or telephone number +44 (0) 1865 884447.

Digital Libraries: Integrating Content and Systems

MARK DAHL, KYLE BANERJEE
AND
MICHAEL SPALTI

Chandos Publishing
Oxford · England

Chandos Publishing (Oxford) Limited
Chandos House
5 & 6 Steadys Lane
Stanton Harcourt
Oxford OX29 5RL
UK
Tel: +44 (0) 1865 884447 Fax: +44 (0) 1865 884448
Email: info@chandospublishing.com
www.chandospublishing.com

First published in Great Britain in 2006

ISBN:
1 84334 155 7 (paperback)
1 84334 166 2 (hardback)

© M. Dahl, K. Banerjee and M. Spalti, 2006

British Library Cataloguing-in-Publication Data.

A catalogue record for this book is available from the British Library.

Typeset by Replika Press, India.
Printed in the UK and USA.

For Mary, Shirley and Beth

Contents

Acknowledgements

The authors of this book are information professionals whose careers have come of age in the Web era. They have had the good fortune to explore, experiment and even achieve a few successes in this exciting environment. However, successful digital library integration can only occur in a supportive environment that offers the freedom to innovate. The authors are indebted to the many individuals that made their achievements possible. Any errors in the book are those of the authors.

Mark is grateful to the mentors that he has had during 16 years of employment in academic libraries, particularly Dennis Hill, Richard West, Louise Robbins, David Bilyeu, Jim Kopp and Elaine Heras. They challenged him and at the same time gave him the freedom to be creative. They also taught him how to be dedicated to the library profession and live a rich life outside of it. He's also very appreciative of the talented colleagues with whom he is currently building a digital library at Lewis & Clark College, especially Margo Ballantyne and Jeremy McWilliams. Above all he is thankful to his wife Mary, who has given him love and support throughout this endeavour while pursuing some ambitious goals in her own career.

Kyle draws inspiration and support from too many people to name here, but he owes Terry Reese a debt of gratitude for extensive technical advice and program code over the years, as well as for keeping him on his toes as a technologist and cyclist. He thanks Stephen Smith for helping him realise how fascinating the guts of a library are, the Oregon State Library for taking a chance on a budding systems administrator, and everyone at the Valley Library at Oregon State University for teaching him most of what he knows about the relationship between people, technology and library operations. Kyle appreciates his dog Keiko for helping him keep things in perspective. He is always amazed how much simpler most problems become after a walk or game of fetch. He hopes his family and friends will not think they are unimportant because they are not listed here – he sees in them the person he would like to become. Most of all, Kyle is grateful to his wife Shirley Lincicum for always being there when he needed her. He will never understand how she maintains her endless patience for him, his many quirks and crackpot ideas.

Michael is grateful to his many Willamette University colleagues and mentors who over the years have shared their ideas, passion, experience and good humour, including Richard Breen, John Balling, John Callahan, and especially Larry Oberg. Joni Roberts and Carol Dorst have provided a sounding board for innovative ideas and a safety net against ill-considered ventures. William Kelm has been a steady and reliable partner in creating and supporting digital library efforts, and Deborah Dancik has provided friendly nudges in new directions. These and other colleagues make Willamette University a creative and supportive community for which he is grateful. Michael's colleagues at Oregon State University, including Shirley Scott and Melvin George, encouraged him to be creative and to see librarianship as a challenging and worthwhile career. Finally, Beth Wilson has shared her love, and her sabbatical, with him during the process of writing this book. He thanks her especially for her terrific patience and support.

List of figures

About the authors

Kyle Banerjee is Library Systems Analyst at the Oregon State Library in Salem, Oregon. He has written numerous articles about digital library issues and is regularly invited to speak about library systems and automation. He is one of the key architects of the state of Oregon's electronic documents repository. Kyle is an avid cyclist and enjoys the outdoors.

Mark Dahl is Assistant Director for Systems and Access Services at Lewis & Clark College's Watzek Library in Portland, Oregon. He has been knee-deep in digital library work for eight years and currently enjoys doing it in a liberal arts college environment. He regularly teaches a distance education course on networked technologies for Emporia State University. For fun he works on his fixer-upper home and explores Oregon's outdoors by running, mountaineering, cycling and windsurfing.

Michael Spalti is Associate University Librarian for Systems at the Mark O. Hatfield Library in Salem, Oregon. For the past ten years he has known the joys of bringing the new language of digital libraries to a liberal arts college and thankfully has been well-received by a tolerant and collegial community. Much enamoured of the Pacific Northwest, he enjoys boating, gardening and cycling (a bit more slowly than others, perhaps).

The authors may be contacted at the following:

Mark Dahl
E-mail: *dahl@lclark.edu*

Kyle Banerjee
E-mail: *kyle.banerjee@gmail.com*

Michael Spalti
E-mail: *mspalti@willamette.edu*

Preface

This book is about the skills and technologies needed to build a digital library. Its purpose is to acquaint librarians, managers and graduate students with what is possible in today's digital library environment. To this extent, the book focuses on tools and strategies. Each chapter introduces current or emerging technologies that have important and practical implications for libraries, suggesting how and why these technologies matter. Our aim is to create a roadmap to significant technologies and how they affect academic and public libraries as they navigate through a period of change.

Throughout the book we explore a relatively new type of library work, in which many different services and information sources are integrated into a single, digital library framework. This task differs fundamentally from those performed by more traditional categories of jobs within libraries, including automation or systems librarians.

Because this new type of thinking is essential to meeting future library challenges, this book will be useful reading for those who manage libraries. It will help library leaders understand the new problems that their organisations must overcome, and the kinds of tools and expertise needed to solve those problems. It will be useful to librarians and library technologists whose work is a critical aspect of solving these problems. Even librarians whose primary job focus is not technological will find that the issues we discuss are important, if not central to their work. Graduate students in library and information science and related fields will also find the book a useful primer on a major aspect of library operations at this time.

The problem of digital library integration confronts all sizes of libraries, and individuals in both large and small settings looking for a broad view of the problems and available solutions will find this book useful. The largest academic libraries often lead the way in digital library work by pursuing some of the more technically advanced forms of integration, but smaller and perhaps more nimble libraries can also do some of the most innovative work. The availability of Internet-based technologies and services makes high-quality digital library integration possible at institutions of all different sizes.

Even though the authors of this book all live and work in the state of Oregon in the Pacific Northwest of the USA, we have attempted to approach the issues from a geographically neutral perspective. Though naturally most familiar with North American institutions, when possible, we also cite examples of work done in institutions in other areas of the world. Most of the technologies, problems, and strategies discussed throughout this book are applicable to libraries across the world.

The book strikes a critical balance between explaining technologies and exploring integration strategies. Library leaders and librarians need to understand how technologies work in order to develop strategies. They need to understand the integration problems that exist and the standards and tools that are available to solve those problems. This book will explain numerous technologies – from web scripting languages, to metadata standards, to digital asset management systems – and then discuss how a library can use them, strategically, to provide an integrated digital library. Because of the broad scope of the book, we will not provide instruction on how to use any particular technology. Rather we will explain its purpose and capability and then move on to associated strategies.

Because of the practical focus of the book, its material is highly topical and ever-evolving. When possible we have attempted to emphasise technologies that have an established track-record and that we believe will have relevance well into the future. Generally speaking, we emphasise integration strategies that are flexible and open enough to adapt to future developments. Because change is a given in digital library integration work, we emphasise strategies that maximise a library's ability to respond effectively to evolving circumstances and new user expectations.

Introduction

Readers of this book already know that libraries are rapidly changing. The print collection, once the undisputed centre of the library, is increasingly marginalised as digital resources meet a growing percentage of research needs. Meanwhile, library users are asking for more sophisticated and well-integrated digital library services. Libraries that cling to traditional service models in an era of new information technology, rising costs and flat budgets cannot thrive. Barely a decade after the World Wide Web began to affect the library and research communities noticeably, old ways of doing library business are shifting toward new professional roles.

The beginnings of this change can be traced back to the early 1990s, when the World Wide Web and hypertext mark-up language (HTML) first made it possible to build a simple digital library from disparate information sources. Creating this early digital library required only a web page with links to the online library catalogue, the electronic resources to which the library subscribed (perhaps initially on an experimental basis) and free Internet resources. Although modest, this small web page was a technological revolution in the making. Earlier mainframe and PC-based library technology had automated the functions and procedures of the physical library. The birth of the World Wide Web began a more fundamental transformation of publishing, entertainment, scholarly communication and, inevitably, library services.

Today, the simple web page of the 1990s no longer meets the needs of most libraries, especially medium and large-sized public and academic libraries. The Internet opens the door to real-time access to resources and services located throughout the world and maintained by numerous libraries, vendors and consortia. This information often resides in constantly changing databases outside the control of library staff. The dynamic nature of digital content challenges libraries to find innovative ways to that address the expectations of users who take for granted the services of sophisticated and powerful websites.

Rather than rely on static web pages and basic services, libraries today need tools for developing such *integrated* digital library services as:

- a clear, well organised and frequently updated portal of electronic resources;

- single username/password access to restricted library services and resources;

- a central point of searching to discover whether the library has electronic or physical access to a particular journal;

- direct linking from a reference to an article to the full text of the article itself;

- 'one click' interlibrary loan requesting that does not require the user to type in the details of a citation;

- online, personal bibliography software;

- dynamically updated databases of resources customised to particular patron needs;

- federated searching across multiple electronic resources;

- searchable repositories of locally managed digital assets including images, documents and sound recordings.

To bring about these and other services, libraries need personnel with skills in both library-specific technologies and more generic web technologies.

Skills and opportunities

In many libraries today, a new kind of technologist is quietly discovering ways to address digital library problems. This person, or persons, understands library operations and library-specific software like integrated library systems, interlibrary loan systems, link resolvers and other content management systems. They also grasp the potential for web technologies to enhance library service.

There is no established job title for these new library technologists. The individuals in these positions are often known as systems librarians, library technologists, digital services coordinators, programmers, systems analysts, web developers and digital librarians, among many other titles. We will employ the title 'digital library integrator' throughout this book when we refer to the library professionals that perform this type of work. The chapters of this book are a kind of primer for digital library integrators and an outline of basic decisions that they and their library colleagues face.

A number of inexpensive and widely adopted 'enabling technologies' make it possible to construct digital libraries. These technologies include the popular, open source Apache Web Server, web scripting languages, such as PHP, Cold Fusion and Microsoft's Active Server Pages. They also include relational databases, such as MySQL and PostgreSQL and other general purpose tools for storing, searching and manipulating information. Together, these enabling technologies allow local libraries to seize control of their digital library environment. Library technologists can use these tools to enhance the digital library, deal creatively with inevitable change and free up the time of other library staff for new tasks in a constantly changing environment.

Beyond enabling technologies, the digital library integrator must have knowledge of critical standards that make integration possible. These standards include generic Internet protocols, such as HTML, XML, LDAP and RSS, as well as library-oriented standards, such as MARC, EAD, NCIP and OpenURL. These two varieties of standards are building a foundation of communication and interoperability that supports digital library integration.

Authentication, identity management and network security are critical areas for digital library integration. Users should be able to log into a digital library with one username and password, preferably the same ones that they use for other functions in an institution, such as a college or university. Identity management allows user characteristics and preferences across a variety of applications, so that, for example, applications, such as electronic reserves and personalised portals, can benefit from 'knowing' about user characteristics, such as what classes they are enrolled in, what they are studying, or their reading preferences. Finally, network security is essential for the integrity and reliability of any digital library. Security concerns increase with the complexity of a digital library and the use of personal information.

Integrated library systems (ILSs) have traditionally performed the functions needed to manage a physical library collection: circulation, catalogue and acquisitions. Increasingly, they are an important component of a digital library. Integrated library system vendors now offer several products to manage digital libraries, such as link resolvers, electronic resource management tools and digital asset management systems. There are also important techniques for integrating the ILS into a digital library: data manipulation within the ILS, interaction between the ILS and external applications and repurposing of ILS data. Traditionally, the ILS has stood at the centre of library technology. As libraries focus attention on their digital presence and as digital library systems become more component based, the centrality of the ILS becomes an open question.

Electronic resource management encompasses acquisitions, collection development and public service activities. It involves interrelated workflows for such tasks as managing licence agreements, administering online access options, and facilitating both the discovery of and access to content. A number of vendors have stepped forward with electronic resource management products that help to integrate workflows and track the electronic content to which a library subscribes. Individual libraries and library consortia have also developed their own systems for managing electronic resources.

Managing repositories of locally created digital content is an increasingly important and relatively new area of activity for libraries. Academic libraries, for example, may pursue a variety of different digital asset management activities, such as digitised photo collections, digitised rare books and manuscripts, curricular materials and multimedia learning objects, faculty research publications, institutional or university press publications and student theses.

Technologies like OpenURL link resolution services have become essential new digital library tools. These technologies provide context aware services, such as linking from a citation to a digital resource that the library has acquired or to an interlibrary loan service. Such linking services dramatically improve the ease with which library research is conducted.

Federated searching allows users to query many different databases simultaneously. Federated search technologies are further complemented and enhanced by aggregation techniques that pre-harvest metadata from multiple sources and provide search interfaces to this content. The aggregation strategy is most obviously represented by Google Scholar, but variations of the approach are gaining ground within the library community, particularly as new harvesting protocols become more widely adopted.

Web portals are, in many ways, the culmination of digital library integration. In its simplest form, a portal may be a library website with links to the library catalogue and external resources. In their more advanced manifestations, portals are highly integrated services. Library web portals may be driven by content management systems that allow librarians to create web pages. They may offer personalised features such as current awareness services and account information. Increasingly, they may use new web technologies like forums, wikis, blogs, RSS feeds and social bookmarking. Portals benefit immensely from custom web programming.

The challenge

Creating and nurturing a digital library requires the proper technological infrastructure. This infrastructure includes servers, application platforms and software applications that diverge from those supported by the information technology department of a library's parent organisation. In order to assure the basic infrastructure and creative independence required to build a digital library, library managers need a clear understanding of the digital library's technical requirements.

Because digital libraries rely on a complex set of network services, they typically operate in an information technology framework created and maintained by other units within the parent organisation. The precise nature of a digital library's technical requirements therefore varies with local circumstances. Specific strategies must adapt to such local factors as the type of directory services, programming languages, operating systems and administrative systems supported by the parent organisation.

Collaborative relationships with other information technology units are thus essential for robust digital library development. These relationships leverage knowledge within the broader organisation, build on existing investment and realise efficiencies. Performing redundant work or developing isolated and idiosyncratic systems has lead to the demise of numerous library automation projects in the past. Relying on vendor solutions insulates the library from this risk and allows staff to focus on solutions to unique digital library challenges.

At the same time, over-reliance on external technology support can stifle creativity, impede change and ultimately disconnect the technology from those whom it is intended to help. It seems unlikely that a robust digital library can be achieved without active engagement by library professionals in the technologies that make it possible. Luckily, the standards and enabling technologies described in this book decrease the need for centralisation by providing accessible, free and relatively transparent technologies, as well as active user communities that provide support and creative ideas.

The digital library integrator is a unique technologist whose expertise is a fusion of information management and information technology skills, a fusion consistent with the historic role of librarianship. Moreover, a digital library is successful when a broad cross-section of library staff is engaged in its design, construction, ongoing enhancement and promotion. To create a thriving digital library service, librarians need to engage technology in the interest of users. Librarians need basic fluency in information technology concepts. With an understanding of digital technology and its possibilities, librarians can participate in creative digital library solutions.

An effective digital library offers services that are highly tailored to the needs of library clientele. A well-constructed digital library enhances the reputation of the library and its parent institution. Finally, the creative nature of digital library development can provide vitality and a sense of pride to those who contribute to the endeavour.

2

Enabling technologies

This chapter will introduce some of the generic technologies that make the integration of digital library services possible. These technologies are either part of the web environment or have been radically altered and reshaped by it. They include network operating systems, web servers, web design, web scripting, web services and relational database management systems. These are the technologies that have empowered libraries to integrate and customise their digital libraries.[1]

Covered in this chapter:

- the web environment;

- network operating systems;

- web servers;

- web design, dynamic web pages, relational databases and web services;

- technology trends.

Before elaborating on each specific technology, it is worth reviewing the broader qualities of the web environment. The Web has revolutionised electronic information delivery in libraries and made digital libraries possible. Web technology, even in its most basic form, offers some profound advantages over the terminal/mainframe and personal computer/ local area network based technologies that preceded it. Though we take these advantages for granted today, they are worth reviewing as we utilise the Web ever more intensively in the digital library environment.

The Web itself has been called a computing platform. The following technical characteristics, while not all unique to the web environment, taken together have made the Web the success that it is today:

- hyperlinking between documents;

- the universality of access provided by the Internet and Internet naming conventions, which give each website and most web pages a unique uniform resource locator (URL) accessible anywhere on the Internet;

- standards for creating (HTML: HyperText Markup Language) web pages and accessing (HTTP: HyperText Transfer Protocol) web pages that allow web browsers on any computing platform to use the Web;

- a client/server architecture in which the client (the web browser) makes requests to the server (the web server) for data;

- server-side computing that can provide web users with access to very powerful computers; for example, the typical individual using Google is utilising a vastly more powerful cluster of computers than they could ever hope to muster at their own home or work;

- client-side computing that complements server-side computing; specifically, JavaScript can make web pages react to user input instantly and, in the case of Ajax (Asynchronous JavaScript and XML), JavaScript can exchange small bits of data with the server to change just a portion of a web page;

- the ability to extend the medium beyond HTML using browser plugins, such as Adobe's Acrobat document reader, Macromedia's Flash Player animation platform and Apple's QuickTime video player.

Aside from these basic technical qualities, we can also identify a set of technical ideals associated with web computing. As individuals, firms and other organisations have used the Web, it has evolved. Various ideas have emerged about how to best exploit the technology. As we discuss the application of web technology to digital libraries, it is worth reviewing what we consider these technical ideals to be, which are by their nature more subjective than factual. They are:

- websites should be platform independent;

- websites should separate their content from their presentation as much as possible;

- data and functionality provided on a website to users should also be available to external web applications, preferably via a web services interface;

- when possible, websites should conform to applicable standards, whether they are generic web standards like HTML and CSS (cascading style sheets) or industry specific standards, such as OpenURL or SRU/W (search and retrieve URL/web).

Even though the basic technical architecture of the Web calls for platform independence, many web pages still work best with a particular browser or operating system. Digital libraries should strive to deliver web services that are platform independent so that their services can reach as many users as possible. Designing platform independent systems also promotes competition in the marketplace for web browsers and computer operating systems.

Websites should separate content from presentation. Basic web pages support text as well as images and may be rendered differently depending on the hardware capabilities and preferences of the individual user. A web page is vastly different from a printed document in that it may be re-sized to fit a viewing screen and viewed with or without images. Often, web pages are designed with fixed sized text and a heavy use of graphical images that impedes easy resizing and use with text-only browsers, wireless devices and screen reading software.

Taking the notion of the separation of content from presentation a step further, the data behind websites should be accessible to other machines on the Internet. A rudimentary way to do this is via RSS feeds, which allow some of the content from one website to be published on another website or within a personal news reader application. A more advanced way to do this is via web services and SOAP (Simple Object Access Protocol). When the data and functionality of a website is available for other machines on the Internet to access, developers can use it to create new web applications that build upon the functionality of the existing site. Amazon is an example of a website that makes its data and functionality available via web services.

Generally speaking, standards are the key to successful web computing. Standards like TCP/IP, HTTP and HTML were essential in formulating the Web. And standards like RSS, CSS and SOAP have extended its possibilities. Standards create a common platform on which competition and innovation can occur. They facilitate the intermixing of components. In the library world, important standards, such as the OpenURL have led to tremendous strides in digital library integration.

In many ways, web services functionality and the adoption of standards are aspects of a broader technological and social phenomenon known as 'Web 2.0'. Generally speaking, Web 2.0 refers to a web that is more interactive both on the level of the software running it and the humans using it. Building Web 2.0 applications often involves combining the data and functionality of more than one website. Making the data behind websites accessible to other machines via standards is essential to this endeavour.

Network operating systems

Services delivered over the Web depend on network operating systems (NOSs) running on server computers. NOSs are computer operating systems designed to fulfil the server role in a client/server environment. Because the Web is based on a client/server architecture, NOSs play an essential role in its existence. Examples of common NOSs include Windows Server, Linux and many different varieties of UNIX. Digital library integrators need to know how to get around the NOS, but do not necessarily need to perform NOS administration.

The NOS has been around much longer than the Web, but the Web has accelerated its evolution and created new uses for it. The Linux operating system is a NOS that has what might be described as a symbiotic relationship with the Web. A global network of volunteer programmers is continuously working to improve it. Both because Linux servers power much of the Web and because the Web facilitates communication among Linux developers, Linux development and usage has accelerated dramatically since the advent of the Web.

NOSs have several characteristics that traditionally separate them from client operating systems:

- the applications that they run are designed to be used over a network;

- they are designed to support multiple users at once;

- they assign different privileges to different users;

- they are designed to be continually available.

In recent years, client operating systems, such as Windows XP and Mac OS X have acquired many characteristics of network operating systems, such as support for multiple users and differentiation of privileges between users. Client operating systems now often share the same base of code with the NOSs marketed by the same company. Nonetheless, companies like Microsoft, Apple and Red Hat still market their NOSs separately from their client operating systems. They generally include a slightly different set of software tools and features with their NOSs.

A NOS can support many important functions in an organisation. These include:

- TCP/IP network infrastructure: NOSs can be configured to act as a router, firewall, DHCP server, or DNS server.

- LAN support: NOSs often perform common local area network (LAN) functions, such as authentication to computer workstations, file sharing and printer sharing.

- Directory server: Directories are a central place of authority about privileges and roles for users on a network.

- Application serving: NOSs can run networked applications including integrated library systems (ILSs) and calendaring software.

- Web serving.

- Relational database hosting for database products like MySQL or Oracle.

Digital library integrators typically perform much of their work within a NOS. Most of this work consists of developing, installing and configuring applications, tuning web servers and designing and optimising relational databases. To perform such work, they need to understand how their NOS of choice handles privileges among users, how to tune it for performance and how it performs critical functions, such as error logging and unattended job scheduling.

Even though digital library integrators need to be able to work within a NOS, they may not need to administer one. Often a library can acquire access to a NOS without maintaining its own server. A parent institution's IT department or an off-site co-hosting service can provide access to a server with the appropriate digital library tools available. If given the appropriate level of access, a library technologist can then use that server to mount and configure the web applications needed for the digital library. The IT department or co-hosting service can then handle the details of backing up the server, applying security patches and otherwise ensuring its overall security and performance.

Nevertheless, many libraries will still find it desirable and necessary to host their own servers and maintain their own NOSs. Sometimes the support available from the parent institution simply will not meet the needs of the library. Sometimes the applications that a library needs to run will fall outside the parameters of access that a central IT department or co-hosting service is willing to offer.

Web and proxy servers

Web servers are the programs running on network operating systems that make web browsing possible. When someone requests a web page from their browser, a web server program delivers that file to them over the Internet. The most popular web servers currently are the open source Apache Server and Microsoft's Internet Information Server (IIS).

Besides simply serving whatever web pages are requested, web servers provide additional functionality to websites. These include:

- organisation of files on a website;

- redirection from one URL to another;

- customised error messages;

- support for uploading and modification of files;

- encryption of sensitive data;

- authentication to sensitive areas of a website;

- support for web scripting languages, such as PHP and Cold Fusion;

- support for special web server extensions or modules.

Web servers provide essential tools for routing users to resources on a website. They can organise files on a website in ways that are logical to external visitors. A single web server program can serve several different websites with different hostnames using a technique know as 'virtual servers'. They can redirect users from one URL on a local website to another location on that site or a location on an external site. They can provide customised error messages and redirection when a user attempts to access a web page that is no longer available.

Using a web server's configuration file, an organisation can create a distributed system for updating and maintaining a website. Individuals can be assigned certain areas of a website to maintain and be given access to only those portions of the site. Using the WebDAV protocol, the web server itself can be used with web editing tools, such as Dreamweaver, to edit content on the website.

Many applications that are crucial to delivering digital library services depend on specially configured web servers. Most web applications used by digital libraries require 'extensions' or 'modules' to be installed on the web server that the library is using. Common modules required by web applications include those that support scripting languages, authentication and data encryption. For example, the popular digital collections system CONTENTdm requires a web server with a module that supports the PHP programming language.

Web servers can authenticate users as they access various areas of a digital library. Web servers can restrict access to content by authenticating using different methods including IP address, cookies or by asking for a username and password. Various web server modules can support username/password authentication by checking them against an LDAP directory, an e-mail server, or a text file of usernames and passwords. Web servers enabled for secure sockets layer (SSL) are able to encrypt connections between the web server and the browser, protecting user identities and passwords.

Proxy servers are basically web servers that act as an intermediary between the web browser and the wider web. The most common use for proxy servers in digital libraries is to provide remote access to IP restricted resources. After the proxy server authenticates and authorises the user, it retrieves the restricted resource using the server's IP address and sends it to the user who is browsing from an un-authenticated IP address. In the past, library patrons had to specially configure their web browser to use proxy servers, but URL-rewriting proxy servers, such as EZproxy that require no browser configuration have now become the norm. Proxy servers are also commonly used to filter access to the Web in public libraries.

Web servers and proxy servers provide a great deal of flexibility in logging activity on a library's website. Separate log files for various areas of a website can be created using a web server and later analysed by log analysis applications, such as Web Trends or the open source Webalizer. Flexibility in logging and analysis is essential for the ongoing evaluation of digital library services.

Many academic libraries host their web pages on servers managed by their parent institution's information technology department. Using a centrally managed web server has similar advantages to using a centrally managed NOS. The library itself does not need to concern itself with the integrity of the web server or ongoing upgrades and patches. The library may also be able to take advantage of an institution's content management system, which might provide templates for web pages that can integrate the library's pages into the design and navigational system of the parent institution's website.

The advantages of hosting a web server dedicated to the library are also compelling. With a web server under its own control, a library can authenticate, secure and redirect content as needed. Furthermore, its staff can install the extensions necessary to test and run the web applications that it requires.

HTML and web design

In addition to system and web server administration skills, digital library integration requires web development skills. Web development encompasses different areas of expertise including HTML/XHTML coding, web page design, web programming (or scripting) and relational database management.

Knowledge of HTML or its more evolved counterpart, XHTML, remains an indispensable skill for the digital library integrator. Even though there are many tools available to generate web pages automatically, there remain many situations in which an understanding of HTML code remains essential.

WYSIWYG (what you see is what you get) editors, such as Macromedia Dreamweaver, Microsoft Frontpage and Adobe GoLive often produce errors in HTML, especially when several edits are made on an existing page. One must possess an underlying understanding of the code in order to correct such errors. Many library specific web applications, including online databases and web OPACs, require snippets of HTML code to configure them correctly. Furthermore, web programmers building web applications with web scripting languages need a solid knowledge of HTML.

Besides these practical applications of HTML, anyone using the Web or building web pages with the aid of a content management system will also benefit from some of the underlying concepts of HTML and web page design. Building a web page with HTML is a fundamentally different process from designing a print document. HTML in its most basic sense describes conceptual parts of a document: the document title, headings, lists, paragraphs, etc. The way that the document is rendered into a page on a browser's screen is the result of a combination of settings determined by the web developer and the local browser.

Inexperienced web developers often build web pages with too little flexibility. They define fonts to be used outright. They fix the size of large portions of their web pages so that they only work best on a certain size of screen. More experienced web developers know how to create pages that work well on a variety of browsers and screen configurations.

HTML has been extended in many ways as the Web has evolved. These extensions include CSS, XHTML and JavaScript. With CSS, the visual style of a website can be defined separately from the HTML code. Using CSS provides an elegant way to change the fonts, colours and layout of a website from a central location. It also allows more flexibility for displaying a web page on the part of the web browser.

XHTML is the more sophisticated cousin of HTML and is currently the recommended way of marking up web pages. Essentially, it has the same purpose and syntax as HTML. However, it conforms to the more strict requirements of an XML document and thus can be processed more easily by a wider variety of devices and applications. Mobile devices, such as smart phones are better able to process XHTML than HTML. For our purposes, we will refer to HTML and XHTML interchangeably.

The most popular way of building a web page still remains straightforward HTML. Some websites, however, use XML to mark up documents and then apply an extensible style sheet transformation (XSLT) to the XML document in order to turn the document into a web page, PDF document, RSS feed, or otherwise formatted document. This configuration allows the website to define its own markup language that is suitable for the types of documents on that site and then transform those documents on the fly to the appropriate format. For example, a digital library website that displays annotated bibliographies could use its own XML document type definition to mark up its bibliographies and then, depending on what a visitor to the digital library wanted, render those bibliographies in HTML, PDF or RSS.

Dynamic HTML or JavaScript provides basic client-side scripting ability for web pages. It is often used to build interactive forms for online web applications. Ajax is a way of designing web applications that permits web pages to act more like a traditional Windows application. On an Ajax-enabled web page, when a user clicks on a button, pulls down a menu, or otherwise interacts with the page, instead of going to the server and reloading the entire page, a bit of JavaScript in the page contacts a web service and updates only the portion of the page that needs attention. Ajax effectively gives websites more muscle to compete with applications that we traditionally might think of as client-only.

Web interfaces are highly graphical endeavours. To build a digital library that is useful and compelling, a library needs to be able to produce user friendly and well-polished web pages. At the outset of the Web, building a web page was still a 'do-it-yourself' endeavour in which anyone with basic HTML skills could create an acceptable looking page. The Web has evolved to the point where libraries should leave the design of their public web pages to those with specific skills in web design.

Web designers need a talent for designing balanced and appealing pages within the flexible context of the Web. To do this, they need skills in the visual arts and technical skills in HTML and CSS. They need to be able to create and manipulate images optimised for the Web using software, such as Adobe Photoshop. Furthermore, they need a user-centred approach that can incorporate input from other stakeholders into their page designs. It is inadvisable to design a website by committee. But the web designer must seek out input from others at all stages of the design process, including inevitable refinements needed after the site is launched.

Sometimes libraries can piggyback the web design work of a parent institution. Indeed, an academic library may be even be required create their web portal using their parent institution's content management system. Often, however, college and university content management systems are not optimised for creating the style of portal required by a digital library. However, an academic library can still borrow fonts, colours, logos and images from their institution's main website to create a portal customised to their digital library needs.

Dynamic web pages

The Common Gateway Interface (CGI) protocol that emerged in the early 1990s provided an essential ingredient for the Web's success. It allowed websites to take advantage of live programs running on servers. The concept of computer programs driving web pages is known as dynamic web pages or server-side scripting. Dynamic web technologies like CGI have made possible many web applications that we take for granted today, such as web searching and online shopping.

There are really two categories of dynamic web page technologies. Server-side *scripting* languages like Perl, PHP, Cold Fusion and Active Server Pages with Visual Basic are processed as they are used (at runtime). They are designed to be easy to learn, work well for simple projects and are commonly used by digital library integrators. More 'heavy duty' server-side *programming* languages, such as Microsoft's C# and Sun's Java are compiled before they are used and designed for building complex, high performance applications with the price of a more complex (and often more expensive) processing environment.

HTML-embedded scripting languages such as PHP and Cold Fusion emerged after CGI in the late 1990s. Whereas CGI scripts have to generate all of the output to the web browser when they are called, embedded scripting language code can be inserted within traditional HTML code. This allows web programmers to write 'static' portions of a web page, such as the header and footer, in straightforward HTML. The script can then produce the 'dynamic' portion of the page (often the result of a query to a database) as the page is accessed. As mentioned above, web servers that support scripting languages usually need to run an extension (such as mod_php for Apache). Support for a web scripting language and a relational database is now commonly included as part of an account on a web hosting service, a sign that server-side web scripting is now considered a near essential part of creating a website.

Figure 2.1 shows PHP embedded in HTML. Notice how the PHP, which starts with the '<?' tag, interrupts the normal flow of HTML to output some data.

Figure 2.1   PHP embedded in HTML

```
<html>
<head>
<title>Sample PHP Page</title>
</head>
<body>
<p>
<?php
echo "Hello World!";
?>
</p>
</body>
</html>
```

Server-side scripting is arguably the digital library integrator's most powerful tool. It can be used to 'glue together' existing systems and to build customised applications. The built-in facilities for working with HTML in languages like PHP make them ideal for extending existing digital library applications or creating new ones. The strong text processing capabilities of many server-side scripting languages make them ideal for working with digital library metadata and textual data submitted by library users. Their ability to connect with many different data sources including comma-delimited files, XML, relational databases, e-mail servers and other web pages gives them the power to integrate various digital library services.

Here are some examples of digital library web applications that can be created using server-side scripting:

- a web portal of digital library resources organised by subject and maintained via the Web by librarians;

- a web application that allows library patrons to browse or search a subset of the content available in the library's OPAC;

- a web page that offers a 'printer-friendly' version of itself in addition to a graphical version;

- a system that allows the template for a library's web pages to be changed in one central location;

- an OpenURL resolver.

In many ways, server-side scripting is also the 'Swiss Army knife' of digital library integration, solving small integration problems and issues as they arise. For example, a server-side script could convert the HTML output of a web OPAC search to an RSS feed. Or a script could check a user's identity before providing a password to an electronic journal.

Web application frameworks build on the functionality of web scripting and programming languages. They provide a comprehensive set of pre-built functions for building dynamic web applications. Typically, they supply tools for accomplishing common tasks, such as accessing and displaying the contents of a database, creating menus and forms and building templates for web pages. Many of them also are designed to build web applications in the 'model-view-controller' (MVC) architecture, which separates the application specific data (model), the display logic (view) and the user interaction (controller) functions of web applications. This architecture allows for changes to be made to the design of a web application without 'breaking' the underlying logic of the application.

Apache Cocoon, Apache Struts, IBM's WebSphere and Sun's J2EE are web application frameworks based on the Java programming language that are designed for very large scale projects. ASP.NET is Microsoft's web application framework and is optimised to work with the C# and Visual Basic languages. The open source Zope framework is based on the Python language and is designed for creating content management systems. It is completely object oriented and all programming is done via a web interface. Ruby on Rails is a relatively new framework based on the Ruby programming languages and allows very simple and rapid development of database-backed web applications using the MVC architecture. Ruby on Rails allows developers to 'scaffold' database-backed applications: a programmer creates a database, Rails extrapolates a basic web application from the database and the programmer customises the application as needed. According to one proponent of the technology, Ruby on Rails programmers can develop web applications ten times faster than they could with conventional web scripting languages (Hibbs, 2005).

A library should pick a primary dynamic web technology to do local integration work that accomplishes the tasks that it needs quickly and efficiently. Small shops should choose a scripting language that is relatively transparent and does not require a complex infrastructure to support. PHP or Perl are popular choices. Even though Perl has been referred to as 'the duct tape of the Web', very large-scale websites, such as Yahoo use seemingly simple, low-tech scripting languages like Perl and PHP to run mission critical services (O'Reilly, 2005).

More advanced web application frameworks, such as those supporting Java and C# provide advantages in performance and coding architecture that are beneficial to organisations with a large base of users and a large team of programmers. Digital library applications designed by a few programmers and subject to a moderate amount of web traffic will not benefit from these more complex frameworks. But even if a library chooses a simple web scripting language for local projects, they may find that they also need to run one of the more complex web application frameworks to support a pre-packaged application that they want to offer to their clientele. For example, the popular institutional repository software D-Space is written in Java and requires a web server enabled to run Java applications.

Digital library shops should make sure that their primary web scripting language has a large user community and a substantial base of software written in the language. This will make it easy to hire people with experience using the language and to find pre-packaged applications written in it. Popular web scripting languages like PHP have a large body of literature about them available and wide communities of support on the Internet. Plenty of utilities and extensions are also an advantage. PHP's PEAR project provides a library of functions that perform commonly needed tasks like database abstraction and XML processing. An integrated development environment, such as Nusphere's PhpED provides a graphical environment for writing and debugging applications.

Web scripting language applications can often be written by individuals with little or no formal training in computer science. A librarian trained in a scripting language can be a very effective designer and coder of a small digital library application as they will have a strong understanding of its intended functionality. In many ways, the beauty of web scripting is that it can empower those with a deep understanding of the need for an application to create it themselves. At an academic library, student employees or student interns can also be an excellent source of programming skill and innovation. As a library's base of web scripts grows, it is important to have someone who can oversee the whole body of code running on the website to ensure that it is robust, secure, well-documented and bug-free.

Relational database management systems

Most web applications depend on relational databases for organisation, storage and retrieval of data. Common web applications, such as content management systems, wikis and blogs, often keep their data in relational databases. Digital library applications, such as portals and digital collections systems, store metadata about the resources that they manage in relational databases.

Relational database management systems (RDBMS) are available in several proprietary and open source manifestations. Oracle and Microsoft SQL Server are common propriety RDBMSs. MySQL and PostgreSQL are the most popular open source RDBMSs. The existence of the Web has accelerated the development of open source RDBMSs, such as MySQL and PostgreSQL, and they are now robust enough to handle very large applications.

Libraries will probably need access to an RDMBS if they are writing or installing their own web applications. They can acquire access to a relational database by installing one on their own server or by accessing one on someone else's server. Web hosting services now often offer access to an open source RDBMS, such as MySQL, as part of their basic package.

Web scripting languages work in concert with relational databases by sending queries to the database and then processing the returned data. Most web scripting languages have the built-in ability to communicate with a variety of RDBMSs. A common strategy when building web applications is to strive for database independence so that an application can be deployed using any one of many RDMBSs.

Figure 2.2 shows the major pieces in a typical web application. Data in a relational database is accessed via a web script and then delivered to the web browser via the web server.

Figure 2.2   The major pieces in a typical web application

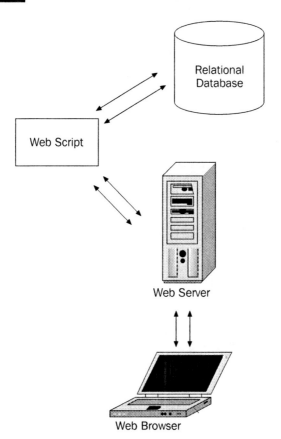

XML, web services, the Semantic Web and 'mashing'

Most people conceive of the Web as something to be navigated, page-by-page, by human beings. An important and growing aspect of the Web, however, is data exchange between computer programs over the Web's protocol, HTTP. Because of its flexibility in representing various kinds of data, XML is fast becoming the most common means by which computer programs perform this type of exchange.

One model of web-based data exchange with particular relevance to digital libraries involves creating large XML files of data and then allowing other applications to harvest and incorporate that data into a search service or index. Archival finding aids marked up in the Encoded Archival Description (EAD) XML schema and posted to the Web using the Open Archives Initiative Protocol for Metadata Harvesting (OAI-PMH) are available for harvesting by digital libraries and search engines. Google Scholar requires libraries to make available their electronic journal holdings in an XML schema to participate in their Google Scholar Library Links program. Digital library integrators, particular those involved in building digital collections, need to know how to create XML documents that conform to such schemas. They also need to know how to create extensible style sheet language transformations (XSLT), rules for transforming the data packaged in one XML schema into another.

'Web services' is a term used to describe computer programs that interact with other computer programs on the Web rather than directly with people. Web services use XML-based protocols, such as SOAP to wrap messages sent from one web application to another. Web services are already available that can enhance digital libraries; for example, Amazon now offers access to much of their bibliographic content as well as customer reviews and images over the SOAP protocol. Google offers limited access to its search engine over SOAP. The new protocol for federated searching SRU/W, utilises SOAP to package search requests to other systems.

The notion of the Semantic Web takes web services to the next level. World Wide Web inventor Tim Berners-Lee envisions the Semantic Web as an interconnected data environment in which computers on the Internet can identify the data available on other websites using technologies, such as the Resource Description Framework (RDF) and the Web Ontology Language (OWL). For example, if one wanted to schedule a doctor's appointment, an automated program could communicate with the Web services of doctors' offices, insurance companies and local mapping systems to find the closest available doctor in the next week that would accept one's insurance (Berners-Lee, 2001). This same type of coordination between disparate systems could lead to more closely integrated digital library services.

Even though we are still a ways away from the Semantic Web that Berners-Lee envisions, already ambitious programmers are 'mashing' together data from various web applications to build new services. For example, one software programmer combined the housing listings on Craigslist.org with Google maps to create an interactive website that shows housing listings in a designated area within a given price range (Anon, 2005).

In some ways, digital library integration currently happens by 'mashing' different systems together. Federated searching systems that surreptitiously connect to several different web-based search interfaces in the background to perform simultaneous searches, web OPAC 'hacks' that enrich functionality in ways vendors did not intend and external databases created from ILS data dumps could all be loosely placed in that category.

To go beyond mashing, or to mash more elegantly, the digital library community must embrace standards. The OpenURL is an example of a simple and effective web-based standard that has led to a tremendous advance in digital library integration. SRU/W and NCIP (NISO Circulation Interchange Protocol) are promising web services standards designed for the library environment. The more that digital library integrators can bring both library specific and generic web standards into the digital library environment, the easier it will be to integrate digital library services.

Software and enabling technology

Libraries can take advantage of these enabling technologies in different ways. First, they can purchase commercial software. Most vendor supplied software that makes up digital libraries including ILSs, link resolvers and digital collections systems runs on these enabling technologies. Library staff members who understand these enabling technologies will be better able to evaluate, select and configure commercial software that utilises them.

Open source pre-packaged web applications are another option. Commonly available software packages include content management systems, wikis, blogs and website search tools. Several open source software packages designed specifically for libraries, and educational environments exist, such as the portal management software MyLibrary, the electronic reserves management system ReservesDirect, and the institutional repository software DSpace. A combination of system administration, web scripting and database management skills are typically required to install and configure these types of applications. Some open source applications are developed and supported through grant-funded entities. Others rely completely on volunteer developers. An active community of support is essential for the success of an open source application.

Libraries can also use these technologies to extend existing commercial or open source software. For example, a web server, web scripting language and relational database might be used in conjunction with an ILS to extend a course reserves module to include electronic reserves. Or a library might customise open source electronic reserves software to fit its own environment.

It is also possible for libraries to use these technologies to construct their own digital library applications. Sometimes it makes more sense for a library to piece together a solution to a digital library problem using generic tools than to purchase a prepackaged application. For example, a library with web scripting expertise might choose to create its own OpenURL resolver and e-journal knowledgebase because of the relative simplicity of the task, the added ability to customise the end product and the cost savings. In other instances, pre-designed software is simply not available to meet a digital library need.

Libraries should be cautious about constructing home-grown applications. Organisations may find it hard to support locally developed software over time, especially with changes in staffing. On the other hand, library administrators and IT personnel tend to exaggerate the drawbacks of writing their own web applications. Technologies like PHP and MySQL are relatively simple and widely understood. Given the ever-changing nature of digital library problems, the stability and potential longevity gained from a vendor solution may not be worth the trade-off in features and customisability offered by a locally designed system. Libraries that reject designing their own software because of a rigid policy that mandates vendor-only solutions do themselves and their patrons a disservice.

Technology trends

The technologies that are critical for mounting a digital library continue to evolve. Some trends are visible in this evolution. First, library technologists need to pay less attention to technologies lower down the technology stack, such as basic server maintenance and network operating system administration. These functions can often be outsourced to a library's parent institution or an outside vendor.

The real work of integration happens higher up the stack in the web space. In many ways, this is a development that parallels what is happening on the business side of the Internet. Major players on the Web, like Yahoo, Amazon and Google, use low-cost open source platforms to run their massive websites. The real value they add happens in the web application software that they use to organise information. Much of this software is written in web scripting languages like PHP. This is also the area in which libraries should seek to concentrate their digital library expertise.

Figure 2.3 illustrates the technology stack. Digital library integration work happens higher up on the stack.

Second, more useful applications and utilities are available to digital library integrators every day. When building a web application, it is

Figure 2.3   The technology stack

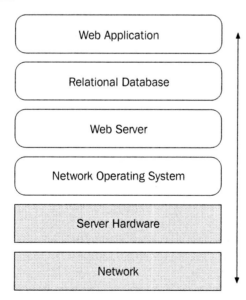

very difficult to do something original. Digital library integrators should scour the Web for pre-built web applications and code libraries that fit their needs before undertaking a project on their own. Libraries that are especially ambitious and innovative might find that initially they need to write their own version of a digital library integration tool. Later, they may discover that a vendor or an open source project has incorporated that functionality into an affordable product and that it makes sense to retire their home-grown work in favour of a prepackaged system.

Third, the increased availability of web services application programming interfaces (APIs), particularly those based on standards, will be the key to further leveraging these enabling technologies. Standards-based APIs like SRU/W and NCIP provide a uniform way of exposing a digital library application's data and functionality. They make greater modularity of digital library applications possible.

Fourth, as the Web has matured, the expectations for the appearance and functionality of websites have increased. Digital library websites are no exception. To meet these higher expectations, libraries need to develop in-house expertise in the above technologies. Where they can, they also need to take advantage of organisational resources, whether it be server support, web templates, or programming help. And they need to strategically acquire digital library products and components to reduce the need to develop things in-house.

Finally, enabling technologies continue to change, and digital libraries must closely monitor that change. There is no sign that we have reached a technological plateau. At the time of writing, Ajax and Ruby on Rails are the hot new web technologies. But there will always be new technologies on the horizon that threaten to shake up the existing paradigm.

As technologies for digital library content delivery evolve, will the creation of an integrated digital library require more or less technological expertise than it does now? This is a question that remains difficult to answer. Because there are so many libraries and content providers out there trying to solve the same problems, we may begin to see the broad adoption of standards that radically simplify the process of creating a digital library. In theory, these standards could make it easy to 'snap together' the tools and content that a digital library needs, without a lot of programming or time-consuming configuration.

On the other hand, several forces may conspire to make designing digital libraries an ever more technical and time-consuming endeavour. Vendors and content providers may continue to favour proprietary systems over standards, thus leaving in place many integration hurdles. New Semantic Web technologies that open numerous possibilities for greater integration may actually make things more complex precisely because they open up so many new possibilities. New formats for digital media and copyright controls could also add to the challenges. Furthermore, digital library users may also continue to increase their expectations for digital libraries that are highly customised to their local institutions.

Summary

- The distinctive technical characteristics of the Web include hyperlinking, Internet naming conventions, platform independence, a client/server architecture, server-side processing, client-side processing, the ability to deliver many different media types.

- Ideally, web applications should follow these rules: platform independence, separation of content from presentation, data and functionality exposed to other applications, support for standards.

- Network operating systems run many digital library applications and digital library integrators perform much of their work using them, but libraries can often acquire access to a NOS without hosting their own server.

- A web server is a software application that runs on a NOS and delivers web content to browsers. Digital library integrators can use web servers to better secure and organise their website and often need to configure them specially to accommodate digital library applications.

- Digital library integrators need a knowledge of the basic building blocks of web pages including markup languages, such as HTML and XHTML, and client-side scripting like JavaScript.

- Professional web design expertise is essential when building a digital library portal.

- Server-side scripting is the 'Swiss Army knife' of digital library integration; it is essential for building customised web applications or tying together existing applications.

- The combination of relational database management systems, such as MySQL and server-side scripting languages, such as PHP creates many possibilities for designing customised digital library applications.

- As digital library systems continue to embrace web standards, more possibilities for highly integrated digital library services will arise.

- Libraries can take advantage of these enabling technologies through commercial and open source digital library software.

- Technology trends central to digital library integration include more innovation in the area of web applications than in other areas of computing, an increasing number of pre-built digital library tools, more applicable standards and more thorough adoption of those standards, increased user expectations for the performance of digital library applications and continually evolving technologies.

Note

1. For an overview of web technologies and their implications for libraries see Rhyno (2003a).

3

The role of standards in digital library integration

People expect a wide variety of services from the library over the Internet. They want to order books, articles and videos. They want to access subscription databases and other specialised resources. Although patrons may think of all these things as library services, they depend on numerous products created by different vendors. Standards allow systems designed for different purposes to communicate with each other so they can interoperate seamlessly. A patron viewing a citation in an index should be able to just click on a link to request it and not have to copy and paste the information into a form. Any library user should be able to see what materials they have checked out and what fines are due without logging in separately into the catalogue and interlibrary loan system. A patron should only have to remember one password to take advantage of library services and it should only take about a minute to change personal contact information. Standards make all these things possible and are essential for integrating local services as well as for ensuring that large-scale cooperative efforts (e.g. consortia catalogues, interlibrary loan systems, etc.) run efficiently.

Covered in this chapter:

■ survey of the most common technical standards used by libraries;

■ structural analysis of key standards;

■ the capabilities and limitations of library standards;

■ promising emerging standards.

Standards are useful for many purposes, but in a library context, they usually perform one or more of five functions: (1) determining content, e.g. the Anglo American Cataloguing Rules specify how to construct valid headings; (2) defining structure, e.g. MAchine Readable Cataloguing (MARC) provides a container that can encode the author, title, publisher and subject of a work; (3) facilitating discovery and transmission of data. e.g. Z39.50 can search databases and retrieve records; (4) authentication, e.g. Lightweight Directory Access Protocol (LDAP) can determine who may access which resources; and (5) displaying information, e.g. HyperText Markup Language (HTML) and cascading style sheets (CSS) are frequently used to format web pages and other documents.

Important library automation standards

As libraries become more dependent on technology and networked resources, they have also become dependent on a vast array of technological standards and protocols. With a few exceptions, integrating systems does not require detailed technical knowledge of specific standards. However, it is important to understand the basic capabilities and limitations of various standards so that realistic expectations can be established for integration projects. As a practical matter, the most important standards relate to authenticating users, searching systems and transmitting data about information resources.

The number of library standards has exploded since the 1990s, but few of them are widely used for significant production work. For the purposes of integrating library systems, the most important standards are currently MARC, a collection of markup languages based on XML (eXtensible Markup Language), LDAP, OpenURL and Z39.50. MARC is used to transfer records, order information, holdings and patron data into integrated library systems; XML provides a syntax that can be used to communicate almost any type of data; LDAP is most often used to authenticate users; OpenURL is used to transfer bibliographic information over the Web (e.g. to generate clickable links in citation databases that allow users to automatically submit interlibrary loan requests); and Z39.50 is a search and retrieval protocol.

There are many other standards with great potential for systems integration in libraries, but as of the time of this writing, their impact is much less significant. Because many of the individual standards that libraries need are complex enough to take an entire book to discuss, this chapter intends only to introduce some key standards necessary to integrate systems and support digital library projects.

MARC

Of the technical library standards, MARC is by far the most widely implemented and has most greatly impacted library services. Because new systems and standards must be able to accommodate the enormous amount of data that already exists, MARC will heavily influence library automation and standards for a long time.

MARC was originally developed by the United States Library of Congress in the 1960s to facilitate the transfer of records on magnetic tape. Although the standard has significant technical limitations and is virtually unknown outside the library community, MARC is still the only practical method of distributing bibliographic records to diverse catalogues and integrated library systems.

When librarians think about using MARC, they normally focus on numeric fields within the record which contain various data elements. However, MARC really consists of three components: (1) the physical structure of the MARC record; (2) the set of tags and markup elements most librarians think about; and (3) the actual data encoded within those tags.

The MARC communications format is a binary structure that holds information. It is similar to tab delimited text and XML files in that syntactical correctness does not depend on field order and content so long as a few special characters are handled properly. Although MARC is used primarily to transfer bibliographic information, it can be used to transfer any type of information that will fit in the structure. MARC is used by many systems to transfer patron information and there is no particular reason why it cannot be used to transfer non-library information, such as recipes or television schedules.

A number of 'flavours' of MARC exist, but they differ in what values are stored in which fields rather than in the physical structure of the record. The various MARC flavours are highly structured, very complex and cannot be used interchangeably without a conversion program. Even when such programs are available, conversion can be problematic because the flavours of MARC reflect different needs being accommodated.

For example, MARC21 uses different tags depending on whether the record in question contains bibliographic, authority, holdings, classification or community information. UNIMARC does not define the same types of records, and even when an analogous record type is available (as is the case with bibliographic records), differing cataloguing practices and concepts make some types of translations difficult because analogous fields are not always present in both types of records. That said, all of the widely used flavours are either derived from MARC21 or UNIMARC. MARC21 is used in most of the English speaking world and was created by merging USMARC and CanMARC (Canadian MARC). UNIMARC and its variations are widely used in Europe and Asia.

Nevertheless, for the purposes of integrating systems, the differences between the various flavours of MARC may or may not be important depending on the need at hand. If the desire is to load vendor records into the online catalogue, the difference is very important. However, if the need is to simply extract or modify a few fields, the systems librarian can easily do this using a number of commercial or free MARC utilities.

Figure 3.1 shows a MARC record for a US government document. Some unprintable characters have been replaced with visible characters to make the record easier to understand. Figure 3.2 displays the same record converted to plain text to make the content easier to read.

A binary MARC record consists of three basic components: (1) the leader; (2) a directory; and (3) the data itself. The leader consists of the first 24 characters of the MARC record. It contains information about the record itself, such as how long it is, the type of record it is and the character encoding for the record.

The directory begins on the 25th character of the record. The directory contains a 12-character entry for each tag in the record. Each entry is structured as follows: the tag is stored in the first three positions, the length of the field in the next four, and the starting address of the data relative to the base address of the record in the remaining five character positions. The base address is where the first field begins. In Figure 3.1, some entries in the directory and the record are shown in bold. The entry '001001300000' means that field 001 is 13 characters long and begins at offset 0000. The entry '24501200209' means that tag 245 is

Figure 3.1 Example MARC record

```
01265cam··2200301·a·450000100130000000300060001300500170001900700140003600800410005
0040003300091043001200124074001400136086003400150088002500018424501200020926001330 0
32930000200046250000550048250000340053750000210057150000450059253301030063765000037
0074065000410077765000450081871000530086371000470091640ocm35690582 40CoLC420020
718143007.04he bmb024bbca4961007s1992 oru b f000 0 eng d4··|aGPO|cGPO|dOCL|dGPO
|dDLC|dMvl4··|an-usp--4··|a0631 (MF)40·|al 53.2:P 12/3|zA 13.92:P12/34··|aBLM-OR-PT-92-26-17
9240 0|aPacific yew comprehensive management strategy|h[microform] :|bfinal /|cprepared by
Pacific Yew Strategy Task Force.4··|aPortland, Or. (P.O. Box 2965, 1300 N.E. 44th Ave., Portland 9
7208) :|bU.S. Dept. of Interior, Bureau of Land Management,|c[1992]4··|a20 p. ;|c28 cm.4··|aDistribut
ed to depository libraries in microfiche.4··|aShipping list no.: 94-0659-M.4··|a"December 1992."4··|a"
BLM-OR-PT-92-1792"-P. [2] of cover.4··|aMicrofiche.|b[Washington, D.C.?] :|cSupt. of Docs., U.S.
G.P.O.,|d[1994]|e1 microfiche : negative.4·0|aPacific yew|zNorthwest, Pacific.4·0|aForest reserves|z
Northwest, Pacific.40|aForest conservation|zNorthwest, Pacific.41·|aUnited States.|bPacific Yew Stra
tegy Task Force.41·|aUnited States.|bBureau of Land Management.4¶
```

Figure 3.2   MARC record from Figure 3.1 converted to text

```
LDR··01412cam··2200361·a·4500
001 ocm35690582·
003 OCoLC
005 20020718143007.0
007 he·bmb024bbca
008 961007s1992····oru·····b····f000·0·eng·d
040 ··|aGPO|cGPO|dOCL|dGPO|dDLC|dMvl
043 ··|an-usp–
074 ··|a0631 (MF)
086 0·|al 53.2:P 12/3|zA 13.92:P 12/3
088 ··|aBLM-OR-PT-92-26-1792
245 00|aPacific yew comprehensive management strategy|h[microform] :|bfinal /|cprepared by
       Pacific Yew Strategy Task Force.
260 ··|aPortland, Or. (P.O. Box 2965, 1300 N.E. 44th Ave., Portland 97208) :|bU.S. Dept. of
       Interior, Bureau of Land Management,|c[1992]
300 ··|a20 p. ;|c28 cm.
500 ··|aDistributed to depository libraries in microfiche.
500 ··|aShipping list no.: 94-0659-M.
500 ··|a"December 1992."
500 ··|a"BLM-OR-PT-92-26-1792"–P. [2] of cover.
533 ··|aMicrofiche.|b[Washington, D.C.?] :|cSupt. of Docs., U.S. G.P.O.,|d[1994]|e1 microfiche :
       negative.
650 · 0|aPacific yew|zNorthwest, Pacific.
650 · 0|aForest reserves|zNorthwest, Pacific.
650 · 0|aForest conservation|zNorthwest, Pacific.
710 1 ·|aUnited States.|bPacific Yew Strategy Task Force.
710 1 ·|aUnited States.|bBureau of Land Management.
```

120 characters long) including the beginning of field marker, indicators and subfields) and begins at offset 209. Because changing any data element changes the record length and directory entries, it is impractical to edit MARC records manually.

Technical challenges when working with MARC

Libraries sometimes encounter problems with invalid records when sending records for authority processing, migrating to a new system, or performing certain tasks because their systems allow storage of data that cannot be converted to a syntactically correct MARC record. Large-scale systems store information in a database which is indexed to meet local needs rather than MARC because searching MARC records directly is both disk and CPU intensive. When records must be output, a program converts the stored information to MARC. If information is stored that violates the technical limitations of MARC, a valid record cannot be created.

The first five digits of the leader in the MARC record contain the length of the record, including the leader and the directory. Because five digits cannot express numbers higher than 99,999, it is not possible to create a valid MARC record that is 100 kilobytes or larger. This limit is sufficient for most practical applications, but libraries often encounter problems when they migrate serials item data within bibliographic records to new systems. If 1,000 items are attached to a bibliographic record and each item contains 100 bytes of data, it is impossible to create a valid MARC record. The directory entries alone consume 1,000 × 12 bytes = 12,000 bytes and the entries themselves take another 1,000 × 100 bytes = 100,000 bytes. As the data and directory entries require 100,000 + 12,000 = 112,000 bytes, the only way to migrate this information is to strip out some of the items and transmit the information separately.

Likewise, the directory structure requires that all field names are three characters long and limits the length of any individual field to 9,999 characters, as that is the largest number that can be expressed with four digits. These limitations constrain flexibility in field definitions and some systems allow storage of extensive holdings or contents notes that exceed the maximum field length, which makes it impossible to create a valid record.

There are other technical limitations to MARC with regards to which characters can be stored, how fields can be structured, etc. Comprehensive technical specifications for MARC records can be found at the Library of Congress MARC Standards website (*http://www.loc.gov/marc/*).

One significant challenge for systems librarians is that it is difficult to work with MARC records using standard tools found on most desktop and server operating systems. To compound difficulties, many vendor-provided services that libraries subscribe to (e.g. linking services from external databases) cannot work with MARC records even though that may be the only input/output option from the catalogue. As a result, the systems librarian must use a program that converts the MARC records to a useful format. MarcEdit is a blisteringly fast MARC utility with a multilingual interface that runs on Windows and UNIX.[1] The MARCpm Perl modules also contain a number of useful functions for working with MARC records. Both utilities are free of charge.

XML

XML is a powerful tool that will heavily influence library technology for the foreseeable future. XML is already ubiquitous. It is used to display information on the Web, pass information between programs, deliver news, configure software and a wide range of other applications.

Despite its name, XML is not a language. Rather, it is a set of rules for creating languages that can be used on any computer. In its essence, all XML does is enclose data within tags. For example, Figure 3.3 shows a valid XML document.

XML does not define tags or indicate what actions should be taken when they are encountered. It only defines rules for structuring tags and data. This means that the tag names and values are arbitrary. Consequently, the choice of 'correct' tags depends on what the program that reads the XML document expects. Detailed information about rules that XML documents must follow can be found at the World Wide Web Consortium XML website (W3 Consortium, 1998).

XML is a subset of SGML (Standard Generalised Markup Language), a markup language that traces its roots back to the 1960s (SGML Users Group, 1990). Markup languages use tags to encode information so that it can be processed by other programs. It is important to note that markup languages do not execute code, manipulate data, display information, or perform any kind of useful work.

Even the HTML used on the Web to display web pages does nothing. Except when viewed through a browser that knows how to interpret the tags, such as Internet Explorer or Firefox, HTML is nothing more than plain text and looks quite a bit like the XML document in Figure 3.3. The value of markup languages is that they structure information in a human readable manner so that it can be used by other programs that interpret the tags. This may not sound like much but it makes even the

Figure 3.3   Example XML document

```
<arbitrary_document>
    <arbitrary_record>
        <arbitrary_field>some field data</arbitrary_field>
        <arbitrary_field>
            more field data
            <arbitrary_subfield>some subfield data</arbitrary_subfield>
        </arbitrary_field>
    </arbitrary_record>
    <arbitrary_record arbitrary_attribute="any value">
        <arbitrary_field>field data</arbitrary_field>
        <arbitrary_field another_attribute="any value" attribute2="anything">
            <arbitrary_subfield subfield_attribute="some value">
                some subfield data
            </arbitrary_subfield>
        </arbitrary_field>
    </arbitrary_record>
</arbitrary_document>
```

simplest documents more versatile, and drastically simplifies information exchange.

When documents are stored as marked-up text, it takes relatively little effort to develop applications that can use and modify the data. Modern desktop and server operating systems contain tools that make it easy to find tags and manipulate data. If a document is stored in a binary format, programmers must write a special application for each type of document. As a result, it is usually much cheaper and easier to work with marked-up data than binary formats.

A number of general and library oriented markup languages have emerged over the past few years. Dublin Core is a minimalist general purpose language that provides basic information about resources. Often, it is necessary to search, display or compare information resources that are structured very differently. Dublin Core makes it possible to drastically simplify records associated with very different types of resources (e.g. books, archival materials, television programmes, reports, etc.) so that they can be searched, displayed and compared with each other. EAD (Encoded Archival Description) is specifically designed to facilitate access to archival materials. Among other things, MARCXML faithfully represents the MARC record without data loss. METS (Metadata Encoding and Transmission Standard) is designed to encode descriptive, administrative and structural information about text, images, video and other materials in electronic libraries. MODS (Metadata Object Description Schema) represents a limited set of MARC21 data using clear English tags rather than numeric ones. ONIX (ONline Information eXchange) is used to transmit book industry product information. RSS (Really Simple Syndication) can pass simple lists and is often used for news feeds. TEI (Text Encoding Initiative) was created to encode literary texts. There are many other XML languages, but they are similar to the ones above in that they allow data to be encoded to support particular types of activity.

The most important differences between various general and library-specific markup languages are in their structure – what types of information they can encode, the granularity of information in the record and what they are optimised to accomplish. For example, unlike TEI, MARCXML and MODS cannot be used to encode entire texts, for the simple reason that they do not have tags that could be used to contain the actual content of a work. ONIX contains special tags that are not present in the other languages that are of special interest to people in the publishing business. For purposes of describing archival material, which is often in boxes in a number of different formats, EAD is far more flexible than MARCXML or any of the other standards mentioned, but it is not an appropriate tool for displaying information on the Web, as browsers do not understand it, nor is it appropriate for encoding entire text. RSS is perfectly suited for displaying brief information, such as headlines, but it cannot be used where a catalogue record with a rich set of access points is desired. Each language has a different purpose and set of capabilities.

To help illustrate the similarities and differences between various languages, the MARC record in Figure 3.1 is represented in Figures 3.4, 3.5 and 3.6 in Dublin Core, MARCXML and MODS respectively. Ellipses in the MARCXML and MODS examples indicate where the records have been abbreviated.

This same record could have been represented using a number of other XML based markup languages. Dublin Core, MARCXML and MODS are similar in that they are all designed to encode brief representations of information resources the same way a catalogue record represents, but does not contain the item described. The 'best' way to encode data depends on how it will be used and what languages the various programs involved understand.

One XML-related standard that deserves special mention is the Simple Object Access Protocol (SOAP). In a library context, SOAP is probably most useful for searching and modifying remote databases, but it also

Figure 3.4 MARC record from Figure 3.1 converted to Dublin Core

```
<?xml version="1.0"?>
<rdf:RDF xmlns:rdf="http://www.w3.org/1999/02/22-rdf-syntax-ns#"
    xmlns:dc="http://purl.org/dc/elements/1.1/">
    <rdf:Description>
        <dc:title>Pacific yew comprehensive management strategy [microform] : final /</dc:title>
        <dc:creator>United States. Pacific Yew Strategy Task Force. </dc:creator>
        <dc:creator>United States. Bureau of Land Management. </dc:creator>
        <dc:type>text</dc:type>
        <dc:publisher>Portland, Or. (P.O. Box 2965, 1300 N.E. 44th Ave., Portland 97208) : U.S.
            Dept. of Interior, Bureau of Land Management,</dc:publisher>
        <dc:date>[1992]</dc:date>
        <dc:language>eng</dc:language>
        <dc:description>Distributed to depository libraries in microfiche.</dc:description>
        <dc:description>Shipping list no.: 94-0659-M.</dc:description>
        <dc:description>"December 1992."</dc:description>
        <dc:description>"BLM-OR-PT-92-26-1792"--P. [2] of cover.</dc:description>
        <dc:description>Microfiche.</dc:description>
        <dc:subject>Pacific yew</dc:subject>
        <dc:subject>Forest reserves</dc:subject>
        <dc:subject>Forest conservation</dc:subject>
    </rdf:Description>
</rdf:RDF>
```

Figure 3.5 MARC record from Figure 3.1 converted to MARCXML

```
<?xml version="1.0" encoding="UTF-8" ?>
<collection xmlns="http://www.loc.gov/MARC21/slim"
    xmlns:xsi="http://www.w3.org/2001/XMLSchema-instance"
    xsi:schemaLocation="http://www.loc.gov/MARC21/slim
    http://www.loc.gov/standards/marcxml/schema/MARC21slim.xsd">
    <record>
    <leader>01354cam a2200337 a 4500</leader>
    <controlfield tag="001">ocm35690582 </controlfield>
    <controlfield tag="003">OCoLC</controlfield>
    <controlfield tag="005">20020718143007.0</controlfield>
    <controlfield tag="007">he bmb024bbca</controlfield>
    <controlfield tag="008">961007s1992····oru····b···f000 0 eng d</controlfield>
        ...
        <datafield tag="245" ind1="0" ind2="0">
            <subfield code="a">Pacific yew comprehensive management strategy</subfield>
            <subfield code="h">[microform] :</subfield>
            <subfield code="b">final /</subfield>
            <subfield code="c">prepared by Pacific Yew Strategy Task Force.</subfield>
        </datafield>
        <datafield tag="260" ind1="" ind2="">
            <subfield code="a">Portland, Or. (P.O. Box 2965, 1300 N.E. 44th Ave., Portland
            97208) :</subfield>
            <subfield code="b">U.S. Dept. of Interior, Bureau of Land Management,</subfield>
            <subfield code="c">[1992]</subfield>
        </datafield>
        <datafield tag="300" ind1="" ind2="">
            <subfield code="a">20 p. ;</subfield>
            <subfield code="c">28 cm.</subfield>
        </datafield>
        ...
        <datafield tag="650" ind1="" ind2="0">
            <subfield code="a">Forest conservation</subfield>
            <subfield code="z">Northwest, Pacific.</subfield>
        </datafield>
        ...
        <datafield tag="710" ind1="1" ind2="">
            <subfield code="a">United States.</subfield>
            <subfield code="b">Bureau of Land Management.</subfield>
        </datafield>
    </record>
</collection>
```

could be used for a wide range of tasks, such as accessing specialised library utilities that automatically get upgraded.

SOAP effectively makes it possible to run applications off the Internet almost the same way they can be run off a local network. SOAP has the additional advantage that it can also be used to break large complicated programs into subroutines that can be processed on different servers simultaneously. SOAP works by allowing computers to execute programs on one another and exchange data using messages written in XML. Although SOAP can be run on any network protocol, it is usually run on the HyperText Transfer Protocol (HTTP), the same protocol as the Web. As HTTP ports are usually not blocked, SOAP can be used in

Figure 3.6 MARC record from Figure 3.1 converted to MODS

```
<?xml version="1.0"?>
<modsCollection xsi:schemaLocation="http://www.loc.gov/mods/
    http://www.loc.gov/standards/mods/mods.xsd" xmlns:xlink="http://www.w3.org/TR/xlink"
    xmlns="http://www.loc.gov/mods/" xmlns:xsi="http://www.w3.org/2001/XMLSchema-instance">
    <mods>
        <titleInfo>
            <title>Pacific yew comprehensive management strategy [microform] :</title>
            <subTitle>final</subTitle>
        </titleInfo>
        <name type="corporate">
            <namePart>United States</namePart>
            <namePart>Pacific Yew Strategy Task Force.</namePart>
        </name>
        ...
        <typeOfResource>text</typeOfResource>
        <originInfo>
            <place>
            <code authority="marc">oru</code>
            <text>Portland, Or. (P.O. Box 2965, 1300 N.E. 44th Ave., Portland 97208)</text>
            </place>
            <publisher>U.S. Dept. of Interior, Bureau of Land Management</publisher>
            <dateIssued>[1992]</dateIssued>
            <dateIssued encoding="marc">1992</dateIssued>
            <issuance>monographic</issuance>
        </originInfo>
        <language authority="iso639-2b">eng</language>
        <physicalDescription>
            <form authority="marcform">microfiche</form>
            <extent>20 p. ; 28 cm.</extent>
        </physicalDescription>
        ...
        <subject authority="lcsh">
            <topic>Forest conservation</topic>
            <geographic>Northwest, Pacific.</geographic>
        </subject>
        <classification authority="sudocs">I 53.2:P 12/3</classification>
        <classification authority="">I 53.2:P 12/3</classification>
        <recordInfo>
            <recordContentSource>GPO</recordContentSource>
            <recordCreationDate encoding="marc">961007</recordCreationDate>
            <recordChangeDate encoding="iso8601">20020718143007.0</recordChangeDate>
            <recordIdentifier source="OCoLC">ocm35690582</recordIdentifier>
        </recordInfo>
    </mods>
</modsCollection>
```

secure environments – at least until it becomes standard security practice to filter all SOAP messages. With SOAP, the programs on the remote servers can be written in any language – C++, Java, Perl, Python, PHP or a number of other choices.

Standards facilitating data discovery and transmission

The Internet transformed library services. Once large numbers of libraries started providing services over the Internet in the 1990s, patron demand for resources maintained by a growing number of geographically and organisationally diverse information providers has been insatiable. Nowadays, libraries often subscribe to dozens or even hundreds of databases. Shared catalogues as well as cooperative licensing and sharing agreements are the norm rather than the exception, and an enormous percentage of what patrons want is not owned by the library. Over a period of just a few years, the primary mission of the library has shifted from preserving information to simply providing access to information managed by a collection of companies, consortia, libraries and other organisations.

These trends present an enormous challenge to libraries wishing to provide good access to their collections. Libraries have historically operated under the assumptions that the library maintains central control of its information resources; that these resources do not change once acquired; and that access to these resources should be provided by a centralised catalogue containing records created by the humans who examined these resources. None of these assumptions is true with a wide variety of network resources.

To provide convenient access to geographically dispersed resources maintained by multiple vendors, libraries need standards which make it possible to interactively query remote databases for different kinds of information resources simultaneously. They need standards that allow people to identify what types of resources a service contains and the ability to request individual items. They need standards that allow patrons to find and retrieve resources without needing to learn the idiosyncrasies of numerous individual resources.

Z39.50

Z39.50 is a robust search and retrieve protocol that traces its roots back to efforts in the 1970s to develop a standardised way to search different databases. It supports a rich set of functions, such as complex Boolean queries, results sets that can be further searched, viewing the status of searches in progress, viewing holdings data, downloading records in different formats and authenticating users.

Z39.50 is a client-server protocol (where an application on an individual computer, opens a connections with a server and retrieves data). What Z39.50 attempted to accomplish with bibliographic records is similar to what modern peer-to-peer networks achieve with music, games and software – a convenient way to share information in a distributed network environment. Z39.50 is maintained by the Library of Congress; a list of presentations, bibliographies, tutorials and documents about the protocol can be found at the Library of Congress Z39.50 website.

Despite the lack of a viable alternative and active support by major vendors, the Library of Congress, OCLC and the library community, Z39.50 has realised little of its potential. The main problem is that Z39.50 is difficult and expensive to implement. It is a complex standard and was not originally intended to run over TCP/IP (the protocol that runs the Internet). Until 2003, the standard was written using obtuse Open Systems Interconnectivity network terminology from the 1980s. To complicate matters, an enormous proportion of functions defined in the standard are considered optional for purposes of determining compliance. As a result, there are many inconsistent Z39.50 implementations, and the standard has failed to become widely used for searching multiple databases simultaneously. Given that it is awkward to implement in a web environment and requires use of ports that standard security procedures block, it is unlikely that Z39.50 will ever achieve great success.

SRU/W: next generation of Z39.50

In recognition that the cost and complexity of implementing Z39.50 had prevented its widespread adoption, the Z39.50 Maintenance Agency at the Library of Congress developed the Search and Retrieve Web service (SRW) and Search and Retrieve URL service (SRU) which are collectively referred to as SRU/W. Although the service differs from Z39.50 in a number of respects, SRU/W incorporates the lessons learned from Z39.50 to provide a powerful search and retrieval protocol specifically designed to work in a web environment.

Like Z39.50, SRU/W supports search sets, complex queries and the ability to ask servers about the resources to which they can provide access. However, the queries sent by SRU/W clients are human readable, as are the XML responses by the servers. SRU/W relies on common web communication protocols and is much simpler to implement than Z39.50

The primary difference between SRW and SRU is that SRW communicates between the client and server using SOAP messages, while SRU uses a URL (i.e. an HTTP GET request) to issue a query and the response is in XML. For example, the following URL can be used to send an SRU Explain request to the Library of Congress test server to find out what services it offers: *http://z3950.loc.gov:7090/voyager?version=1.1&operation=explai.*

Figure 3.7 shows the response from the server – ellipses indicate where the record has been abbreviated. It shows what indices are present, features and other information useful for helping the client interoperate with the server.

Among other things, the response from the server indicates that a subject index is present. Therefore, the URL: *http://z3950.loc.gov:7090/*

Figure 3.7 **Response from Library of Congress Server to SRU Explain request**

```xml
<?xml version="1.0" ?>
<zs:explainResponse xmlns:zs="http://www.loc.gov/zing/srw/">
    <zs:version>1.1</zs:version>
    <zs:record>
        ...
        <zs:recordData>
            <explain xmlns="http://explain.z3950.org/dtd/2.0/">
                <serverInfo>
                    <host>z3950.loc.gov</host>
                    <port>7090</port>
                    <database>voyager</database>
                </serverInfo>
                <databaseInfo>
                    ...
                </databaseInfo>
                <indexInfo>
                    ...
                    <index id="4">
                        <title>title</title>
                        <map>
                            <name set="dc">title</name>
                        </map>
                    </index>
                    <index id="21">
                        <title>subject</title>
                        <map>
                            <name set="dc">subject</name>
                        </map>
                    </index>
                    ...
                </indexInfo>
                <schemaInfo>
                    ...
                    <schema identifier="info:srw/schema/1/dc-v1.1" sort="false" name="dc">
                        <title>Dublin Core</title>
                    </schema>
                    ...
                </schemaInfo>
                <configInfo>
                    <default type="numberOfRecords">0</default>
                </configInfo>
            </explain>
        </zs:recordData>
    </zs:record>
</zs:explainResponse>
```

voyager?version=1.1&operation=searchRetrieve&query=subject=z39.50&
startRecord=3&maximumRecords=1&recordSchema=dc could be used
to retrieve the third record in a response set for books containing the
subject word 'Z39.50' in Dublin Core XML. Figure 3.8 shows the
response from the server. Note that the server indicates that four records
matched the query even though only one was retrieved.

SRW is very similar to SRU, except it uses SOAP messages instead of
URLs to retrieve data. Figure 3.9 shows an Explain request encapsulated
in a SOAP message.

Figure 3.8 Response from Library of Congress Server to SRU Subject Query for 'Z39.50'

```
<?xml version="1.0" ?>
<zs:searchRetrieveResponse xmlns:zs="http://www.loc.gov/zing/srw/">
    <zs:version>1.1</zs:version>
    <zs:numberOfRecords>4</zs:numberOfRecords>
    <zs:records>
        <zs:record>
            <zs:recordSchema>info:srw/schema/1/dc-v1.1</zs:recordSchema>
            <zs:recordPacking>xml</zs:recordPacking>
            <zs:recordData>
                <srw_dc:dc xmlns:srw_dc="info:srw/schema/1/dc-schema"
                        xmlns:xsi="http://www.w3.org/2001/XMLSchema-instance"
                        xmlns="http://purl.org/dc/elements/1.1/"
                        xsi:schemaLocation="info:srw/schema/1/dc-schema
                        http://www.loc.gov/z3950/agency/zing/srw/dc-schema.xsd">
                    <title>Information retrieval (Z39.50) : application service definition and
                        protocol specification : an American national standard /</title>
                    <creator>National Information Standards Organization (U.S.)</creator>
                    <creator>American National Standards Institute.</creator>
                    <type>text</type>
                    <publisher>Bethesda, Md. : NISO Press,</publisher>
                    <date>2003.</date>
                    <language>eng</language>
                    <subject>Z39.50 (Standard)</subject>
                    <subject>Library information networks</subject>
                    <subject>Information storage and retrieval systems</subject>
                    <subject>Computer network protocols</subject>
                    <identifier>URN:ISBN:1880124556 (alk. paper)</identifier>
                </srw_dc:dc>
            </zs:recordData>
            <zs:recordPosition>3</zs:recordPosition>
        </zs:record>
    </zs:records>
</zs:searchRetrieveResponse>
```

Figure 3.9 Example of SRW Explain request

```
<SOAP:Envelope xmlns:SOAP="http://schemas.xmlsoap.org/soap/envelope/">
    <SOAP:Body>
        <SRW:explainRequest xmlns:SRW="http://www.loc.gov/zing/srw/">
            <SRW:version>1.1</SRW:version>
        </SRW:explainRequest>
    </SOAP:Body>
</SOAP:Envelope>
```

As of this writing, SRU/W is still so new that there is little support for it in the vendor or library communities. However, because the barriers to implementation are relatively low, it has a rich set of functions that will work much better in a web environment than Z39.50. In addition, as it is maintained by the same agency within the Library of Congress that is charged with maintaining Z39.50, the prospects for good support for SRU/W are good.

OpenSearch

OpenSearch (*http://opensearch.a9.com/*) is like SRU in that it is used to find materials that match a particular information need, allows clients to ask a server how queries can be constructed, and passes searches using URLs. OpenSearch is different from SRU because it was developed by a private company, is simpler to implement and returns the results in RSS or atom that can be read with a newsreader. OpenSearch is intended for any kind of media, including still images, audio and video. Despite its minimal functionality, support in the vendor community for OpenSearch has grown rapidly. Major organisations, such as Amazon, a number of major newspapers around the globe, the US National Library of Medicine and a variety of web-based information providers respond to OpenSearch queries. A large number of blogs, services and minor information providers also support OpenSearch.

Open archives initiative

The Open Archives Initiative (OAI) helps provide access to multiple digital collections by providing a framework that allows libraries and other service providers to harvest metadata about collections according to rules specified in the Protocol for Metadata Harvesting (PMH). Once a library or service provider downloads metadata about a collection, it converts this information to a searchable centralised database. The effect of this process is to allow users to search multiple collections simultaneously. OAI is maintained by an independent steering committee and support for it comes from the Digital Library Federation and Coalition for Networked Information.

At first glance, the purpose of OAI may seem very similar to Z39.50 or SRU/W. However, it is very different in that OAI-PMH requests data in bulk, while Z39.50 and SRU/W are designed for tightly defined interactive searches. OAI is not designed to allow users to interactively search for items that meet a specific information need. Rather, it only provides a simple framework that allows organisations to download batches of records from an archive. OAI is designed to be easy to implement and it should take less than a day for an experienced programmer to set up a web server to respond to OAI-PMH requests.

It is important to be aware that despite its name, OAI only provides access to metadata about resources – it does not provide the resources themselves. Also, the 'Open' in OAI refers to the openness of the architecture. It leaves policy matters, such as access control and fees to those who provide the services. OAI requires support for Dublin Core, but OAI metadata providers may support other formats that meet the needs of specific communities as they see fit.

OpenURL

Like SRU, OpenURL is a simple protocol that uses a URL to request items. Unlike SRU, the purpose of OpenURL is to supply information for a specific item, while SRU is designed to request an unknown number of items to meet an information need. OpenURL has widespread support in the vendor community and is used for tasks ranging from providing links in citation databases, allowing users to request items via interlibrary loan with a single click, to connecting from catalogue records to articles in full text databases.

In its essence, OpenURL defines a few fields that transmit bibliographic information to a web server. An OpenURL request might look like: *http://openurlresolver.edu/?sid=Test%System_ID&genre=article&issn= 0000-0000&atitle= Any%20Article%20Title&title=Name%20of% 20Journal&volume=1&issue=1&aulast=Author_Surname&aufirst= Author_Given_Name.*

OpenURL's success is largely a function of its simplicity. However, it can only be used to transmit limited bibliographic information, though the standard is extensible and by transmitting a digital object identifier one can theoretically access any useful information about a resource and connect to it with proper access permissions. Programs that direct

OpenURL requests can be directed to appropriate services (known as OpenURL resolvers) can readily be purchased, though libraries often develop their own. OpenURL is so simple that a basic resolver can be designed in as little as a few hours.

Digital object identifiers

Digital object identifiers (DOIs) can be thought of like an ISBN or UPC because they are strings of case insensitive characters that uniquely identify a resource. A DOI consists of two parts: the prefix and the suffix. As is the case with ISBNs, an agency wishing to issue DOIs must register to obtain a prefix and than can issue unique suffixes to individual resources as it chooses. All resources which are assigned DOIs by an agency have the same prefix but the prefix does not change if ownership of the resource is transferred to another agency. DOIs do not have to follow any particular pattern except that all prefixes begin with '10'. DOIs do not contain a set number of characters, are not required to have any meaning or contain check digits, though there is nothing to prevent the issuing agency from creating DOIs that are derived from meaningful values or which contain check digits.

If an agency were issued the prefix '23456' and wished to assign the suffix '1234567890ABCDEFG' to a resource, the resulting DOI would be: 10.23456/1234567890ABCDEFG.

Likewise, if the same agency wished to assign the DOI and the resource above was associated with ISBN 1-234567-89-X, the following would also be a perfectly legitimate DOI: 10.23456/ISBN1-234567-89-X.

Once a DOI has been assigned, it can be transmitted to a DOI resolution service to obtain the network address of the resource or other relevant information and services. It is important to be aware that DOIs do not replace OpenURLs or vice versa. Rather, they are complementary technologies and can be used in conjunction with a local resolution service to allow users to access a resource. For example, a DOI could be embedded in an OpenURL request and, similarly, a DOI resolution service could use a DOI to generate an OpenURL request to a library's interlibrary loan system or a vendor database.

Authentication standards

As the number of network resources that libraries provide access to grows, it becomes increasingly important to provide standards so that services can readily determine who has what access to which materials. Local and remote users need access to databases. Users want to request materials via interlibrary loan, check their patron records in the catalogue, send jobs to a network printer, use their wireless laptops and perform other functions. Issuing separate usernames and passwords for each service is completely impractical because adding, deleting or modifying users becomes unwieldy. When library services can employ standard authentication methods, services for users can be improved while reducing staff and hardware costs.

Lightweight directory access protocol

There are many authentication protocols, but LDAP is one of the best supported methods to control access. As its name implies, LDAP is a protocol that specifies how directory information can be queried and manipulated. LDAP is essentially a simple version of the complex X500 directory service (hence the 'Lightweight' component in the acronym LDAP). LDAP has become the standard for providing e-mail, phone and directory information.

That said, LDAP's most important function is to authenticate users. Many products, such as catalogues, proxy services, wireless access points, or interlibrary loan software can use LDAP to see if an individual is authorised to use a resource.

It is important to be aware that most library products that support LDAP use the protocol only to validate users. They usually cannot transfer address information from the LDAP server to other services that maintain their own patron databases, such as the OPAC or interlibrary loan system. Therefore, if a patron changes their address, this information still needs to be changed in multiple places unless the process of sending the changes to all systems can be automated.

Shibboleth

Shibboleth allows multiple institutions to share authentication information without revealing personal information. Shibboleth works when a group of institutions agree to grant access to each others' resources based on user attributes rather than personal information. For example, faculty or students majoring in a particular discipline would be attributes. When a restricted access website needs authentication information, it goes to Shibboleth, which then redirects the request to the user's home institution. The home institution asks for a user ID and password, and Shibboleth generates a temporary name for the user. The restricted access website does not know who the temporary name represents, only that it was issued by a trusted institution. The website then asks the home institution for the unknown person's attributes. If they are acceptable, access is provided.

Shibboleth allows users to access resources maintained by other institutions without the need for a different username or password or a proxy server. At the same time, Shibboleth protects the anonymity of users preserving both privacy and reducing the risk of identity theft. Although Shibboleth is designed to be relatively easy to implement, it has relatively little support in the vendor and library communities, and most interest in Shibboleth is among a relatively small number of major academic institutions.

Standards facilitating particular processes

There are too many standards associated with particular library operations to enumerate, but library managers and systems personnel need to be aware of those that have significant potential for improving service and/ or reducing cost. For example, the NISO Circulation Interchange Protocol (NCIP) defines a two-way communication process that supports circulation and interlibrary loan operations, such as patron and item enquiry, check-out, check-in, renewal and other useful transaction processes. Because NCIP automates what is normally a cumbersome manual process, NCIP has enormous implications for operations, such as patron initiated interlibrary loan, integrating systems produced by different vendors, borrowing between consortia partners, or self-service kiosks.

Unfortunately, NCIP is still relatively new and many products either do not support it at all or do not yet implement many of its features.

A related protocol, ISO-ILL lacks many features of NCIP, such as the ability to locate and check the status of items. However, ISO-ILL is supported by major interlibrary loan products, and it allows libraries using different proprietary systems to send and receive interlibrary loan requests. Aside from facilitating the request process, ISO-ILL makes it possible to automate administrative functions such as transmitting billing information.

It is important to be aware that some standards are intended for use within other standards. For example, the title in a MARC21 bibliographic record is constructed according to rules in the Anglo American Cataloguing Rules (AACR), which in turn conform to International Standard Bibliographic Description (ISBD) punctuation rules. Likewise, ISO-ILL requests may include messages that conform to the Electronic Data Interchange for Administration, Commerce and Transport (EDIFACT) transfer syntax. EDIFACT is designed to facilitate e-commerce and defines messages and their contents. It does not specify how the messages are sent, so this can be left to individual applications.

Emerging standards

In recent years, technology has advanced very rapidly and new standards constantly emerge to meet current or anticipated needs. For example, in response to the growing need for libraries to analyse usage statistics across databases maintained by different content providers, representatives from the vendor and academic communities embarked on the Standardized Usage Statistics Harvesting Initiative (SUSHI). SUSHI defines a way for libraries to automatically harvest usage data in a standard format (NISO SUSHI Working Group, 2005).

Project managers embarking on digital library projects must always be cognisant that the value of a standard is measured by its acceptance, and that it is extremely risky to rely on standards with little support in the marketplace. Useful, elegant and highly functional standards often fail. The QWERTY keyboard and MARC format are just two examples where arcane, technically inferior standards have endured while vastly superior ones failed. These are not anomalies – there are countless examples where seemingly useful library standards failed and the result has been the loss of huge amounts of data because hardware (e.g. tape, e-book, disk, etc.) or file formats became obsolete.

Libraries will inevitably implement new standards and technologies. MARC is still the most widely supported library standard and will continue to be very important for a long time. For this reason, any new data retrieval standards that libraries adopt must be able to take advantage of the enormous amount of existing information stored in MARC, while being flexible enough accommodate new types of information that have not yet been invented.

Ever since the XML standard was first approved in 1996, predictions have been made that it will replace MARC. As library services become increasingly web-based and patrons increase reliance on tools that search many other resources at the same time they search the catalogue, such a transition seems almost inevitable. Working with binary MARC information in a web environment is simply very awkward from a technical perspective. XML, SOAP and related technologies make tasks, such as integrating systems and services relatively easy and enjoy strong support outside the library community.

However, a number of practical hurdles must be overcome before libraries will use XML for tasks that have been accomplished with MARC. Libraries have to agree on how records would be encoded in XML. For example, if libraries share data in MARCXML rather than MARC, they would still be committed to tracking hundreds of fields, subfields and indicators. In other words, the records would still be time-consuming to create and unreadable by anyone who cannot already interpret MARC. If MODS, Dublin Core, or some other scheme is used, librarians must be willing to agree that data elements that cataloguers have been faithfully creating for decades are unnecessary. Even though many of these data elements (e.g. fixed fields describing things, such as tape size for sound recordings, whether or not the book is a festschrift, whether maps are included, etc.) are typically ignored by catalogues, resistance to any record scheme that does not retain this information should be expected. Once librarians agree on an alternative to MARC, it will take a great deal of time and money for bibliographic utilities, vendors and libraries to modify their systems.

That said, the migration to XML can be accomplished while maintaining compatibility with legacy systems and without data loss. For example, the Evergreen open source catalogue developed by the Georgia Library PINES programme stores a copy of each record in MARCXML (Evergreen Development Team, 2006). The information is indexed as the system needs, but it can be easily converted into other formats to facilitate information sharing. By storing the record in MARCXML, all information is retained and MARC records can be generated if necessary. At the same time, Evergreen can easily be modified to accommodate data in other formats, such as MODS or Dublin Core.

It is important to keep in mind that all standards are ultimately implemented by people, and it is people rather than tools (i.e. standards and technologies) that solve problems. For this reason, standards that make a great deal of technical sense are sometimes difficult to implement. Even when it comes to creating simple documents on the Web, humans are more interested in a compelling visual presentation than in formatting codes. For this reason, building well-structured collections that can be easily searched and accessed via well-conceived communication and authentication protocols is much more than a matter of developing easy-to-use tools. Vendors will not invest the money to support a standard that is not widely used, and no one can use a standard that lacks support. However, when standards are useful but simple to implement, they can gain widespread acceptance very quickly.

Summary

- In a library context, standards are important for determining content, defining structure, facilitating discovery and transmission of data, authentication and displaying information.

- For purposes of integrating library systems, the most important standards are currently MARC, a collection of markup languages based on XML, LDAP, OpenURL and Z39.50. However, SRU/W appears to be a very promising alternative to Z39.50.

- DOIs make it possible to uniquely identify resources. DOIs can be used in conjunction with OpenURL and other standards to obtain access to networked resources.

- MARC is by far the most widely supported standard and it has profoundly influenced systems, services and workflow in libraries of all sizes. For this reason, MARC will continue to be a very important standard for many years.

- XML is essentially a set of rules for creating languages. By itself, XML cannot execute code, manipulate data, display information, or perform any kind of useful work.

- As library services become more distributed across diverse systems, standards that facilitate searching of remote systems and transferring data will grow in importance.

- User-friendly authentication methods are critical to providing convenient service. LDAP is the most widely supported authentication method.

- The value of a standard is measured by how well it is supported more than its technical merits. It is risky to implement systems that rely on emerging standards, because they may not be supported in just a few years.

Note

1   See the MarcEdit homepage: *http://oregonstate.edu/~reeset/marcedit/ html/* (accessed: 17 February 2006).

4

Authentication, identity management and security

The goals surrounding authentication, authorisation, identity management and security are relatively universal in the web environment. Users need to be able to access services from anywhere. They should only need to remember one username and password. When they change their names, addresses, passwords, etc., they should only need to do this once in one place. Users should be able to establish profiles in various applications that follow them around wherever they access each application. Services should be reliable and easy to use, but clients should only be able to access services they are authorised to use. Systems that contain user information, intellectual property and financial data should be safe from internal and external threats.

Covered in this chapter:

- the importance of authentication, authorisation and identity management in digital libraries;

- ILS, LDAP and locally developed approaches;

- data, network and server security;

- preventing and responding to security breaches in digital library systems and library networks,

Digital libraries need robust authentication, authorisation and identity management to provide convenient, integrated services. Authentication identifies users and ensures they are who they claim to be. Authorisation is the process that determines whether an authenticated user may access a particular resource or perform some action. Identity management makes it possible to customise the library experience for each user and make library services more convenient.

The goals surrounding authentication, authorisation and identity management have not been achieved in the web environment as a whole. Web users are frequently expected to maintain separate accounts for merchants, financial institutions, publications, healthcare providers, colleges and universities as well as digital libraries and other organisations. Typically, users create an account and provide personal information, such as address and phone number. They cannot establish that a website is trusted and automatically provide it with personal data and a facility for authentication/authorisation. The problem of providing secure identity management has been recognised for years, but none – including Microsoft's well-funded and supported Passport initiative – have succeeded. Currently, the Liberty Alliance organisation is working to develop a federated identity management solution based on open standards that might solve some of these problems.

Given that they are generally maintained by a single organisation, digital libraries should be able to achieve the authentication and identity management goals that are elusive in the wider web environment. Even in such a limited context, however, providing effective authentication, authorisation and identity management is difficult. Libraries typically use completely separate products to check out materials, request items via interlibrary loan (ILL), access research databases remotely, connect to a wireless network, use library workstations and perform a number of other functions.

Digital library applications usually require four types of data associated with their users:

- Authentication data that can verify that the person is who they say they are. This commonly takes the form of a username and password.

- Authorisation data that confirms that a person holds a certain status within an organisation that allows them to access particular resources. In an academic environment this often translates into student, faculty, staff, etc.

- Generic data about users needed by multiple systems: this typically includes addresses, phone numbers, etc.; in an academic environment, it might also include courses in which an individual is enrolled or teaches.

- Application specific data: this is data specific to a particular digital library application. It could include checkout data in an ILS or interlibrary loan system, a set of URLs in a personalised portal application, or a set of digital image records in a digital asset management system.

Most library software products that offer personalised services including ILS OPACs, interlibrary loan systems, MyLibrary-style web portals, etc. have the capability of keeping all of this data in their own distinct silo. A typical ILS or interlibrary loan system retains addresses and phone numbers of patrons as well as data about what each patron has checked out. It stores usernames and passwords for authentication. The problem with this scenario is that it is hard to synchronise the data elements that are common to multiple systems. Even if library staff add users to all systems at the same time as they sign up for services, any changes to user records become problematic because staff must remember to make changes in all systems.

Fortunately, many digital library applications permit external authentication and authorisation using various methods. These methods include validating username and passwords against the ILS, a Lightweight Directory Access Protocol (LDAP), e-mail or File Transfer Protocol (FTP) server, Remote Authentication Dial In User Service (RADIUS), Shibboleth, Athens, the Standard Interface Protocol (SIP), or even a simple text file of username and passwords. External authentication/authorisation effectively allows libraries and their parent organisations to centralise usernames and passwords in one place, thereby giving users the opportunity to change their passwords in one place.

Centralising authentication/authorisation does not help synchronise data such as addresses, phone numbers and materials checked out across systems. In some cases, this is not a problem. Proxy servers and basic electronic reserves systems may only need to authenticate and authorise users. However, more complex applications, such as interlibrary loan or circulation modules that need to send overdue notices or perform other tasks may need addresses, phone numbers and application-specific data, such as a circulation list of materials checked out, fines due, or application preferences. Ideally, these kinds of applications could store data common to multiple applications in an external, centralised source like an LDAP directory. Unfortunately, many digital library applications are not capable of reading common data from an external source.

Integrated library system approaches

Using the ILS to store authoritative patron data is a good option for libraries willing to purchase most of their major services through their ILS vendor. This approach is normally more expensive than alternatives, but it may be an appropriate option for libraries with limited technical staff. The advantage of ILS-based services is that they tend to be well-integrated and changes to user records do not need to be propagated to other systems. The disadvantage of relying on the ILS for proxy, interlibrary loan, federated search and other types of services is that the ILS products may cost more and lack the functionality of products from other vendors.

Third-party applications can sometimes use ILS-based authentication to validate users from the ILS user database. ILS vendor APIs vary widely in functionality. Most only allow for authentication and read access to user data. Some require a control number to access a particular patron record. Most do not allow data to be updated.

LDAP solutions

Although most people think of LDAP as a directory, it is by far the most widely supported authentication and authorisation mechanism for digital library applications. It is available for all major operating systems and can be run on inexpensive hardware. LDAP can be set up relatively quickly and easily, as most large organisations, like colleges, universities or city government, already have an LDAP server.

Technically, LDAP is an information model with a protocol for querying and updating it.[1] In other words, LDAP is a database that is optimised to contain directory information that can be read very quickly. Typically, this includes commonly needed data about people, such as phone numbers, addresses, etc. It also often includes data about any groups to which a person belongs within an organisation: if they are part of a certain department, enrolled on a particular course, etc. This data can be useful when building customised digital library services. LDAP should not be confused with relational databases, because it is designed to perform only certain kinds of operations efficiently to minimise the system and staff resources to maintain the service.

It is important to be aware that digital library products that claim 'LDAP compliance' offer varying degrees of functionality with external LDAP directories. LDAP compliance does not ensure interoperability because guidelines in the standard can be interpreted differently. More importantly, LDAP compliance is typically claimed when an application only has the ability of reading an LDAP directory but not the ability to insert, modify or delete entries.

This means that many library products that claim LDAP compliance can use LDAP for authentication, but cannot do anything else – this significantly reduces the value of LDAP support. For example, a proxy server that can use LDAP for authentication but not authorisation, could not limit access to an expensive specialised database that only supported one concurrent session to users with a certain attribute in an LDAP directory, such as graduate or faculty status. At the time of this writing, major ILS and interlibrary loan products with LDAP support could only authenticate users with the same username and had no ability to extract or update patron information. As a result, if a library had an ILS and interlibrary loan system that validated using a campus LDAP server and a student changed their address, it would still be necessary to change the address in the ILS and interlibrary loan systems.

Many other web applications, such as blog software, digital collections systems and electronic reserve systems use LDAP for authentication and authorisation. Most of them use LDAP to check a username/password combination. They create a user account with the same username as the LDAP server and then save application specific data for the user within the application. Typically, they use LDAP for authentication each time a user logs in, but keep all other data about the user within their system. LDAP makes it very easy to add web applications where some level of authentication is desirable, such as homepages or wikis, where employees or library patrons can immediately log in with a familiar username and password. Home-grown web applications can similarly take advantage of LDAP for authentication, authorisation and extracting user data, because web scripting languages, such as PHP have built-in functions for easily accessing LDAP directories.

It normally takes only modest programming skills to distribute LDAP information to any service. LDAP servers contain utilities that allow data to be exported, imported and manipulated. The popular OpenLDAP utilities ldapadd, ldapdelete, ldapmodify and ldapsearch allow entries in an LDAP server to be added, deleted, or modified. Slapadd and slapcat allow systems administrators to add multiple entries or convert the entire directory to a plain text LDAP Interchange Format (LDIF) file that can be propagated to other services.

Figure 4.1 shows an example LDAP record in LDIF format. Each line in an LDIF file begins with an attribute name and a colon followed by the value of the attribute. The Distinguished Name (dn) is special attribute that must be unique for each record, but the required and optional attributes allowed for a particular entry are defined in the LDAP server's

| Figure 4.1 | Example LDAP record in LDIF |

```
dn: uid=doej, ou=people, o=myuniversity.edu
objectclass: top
objectclass: person
objectclass: organizationalPerson
objectclass: inetOrgPerson
cn: John Doe
sn: Doe
givenname: John
uid: doej
ou: library
ou: people
description: Example person
telephonenumber: 555-5555
userpassword: {sha}bs9Qsjfapbd9ce
```

object class structure. This means that different LDAP servers may store different attributes about different kinds of objects, although best practices exist for establishing which attributes should be associated with certain common types of objects, such as people.

Shibboleth

Shibboleth is a web-based protocol that allows institutions to authenticate and authorise each others' users, so it is an appropriate tool when libraries want to share resources on a limited basis.[2] Shibboleth discloses only those attributes about a patron that are necessary for the authenticating agency to decide whether access should be granted. For example, consortia can use Shibboleth to authenticate users for cooperatively purchased electronic resources. It is also an appropriate tool for universities seeking to limit access to electronic preprints or special collections to faculty and students from other universities.

It is important to be aware that Shibboleth does not actually perform authentication, so it should not be seen as a replacement for LDAP or other authentication methods. Rather, it defines a set of protocols for exchanging user information. Shibboleth user authentication is completely dependent on the procedures used by the institution providing the user identities, though LDAP is the most likely possibility. Setting up Shibboleth requires relatively advanced system administration skills, so it is an appropriate authentication method primarily for larger institutions that need to be able to grant access to each others' users.

Athens

Athens is a system used primarily in the UK that permits users to access local and external resources with a single username and password. It is similar to Shibboleth in that it can be used for identity management and authentication to access resources. However, Athens is fundamentally different from Shibboleth in that it performs authentication and authorisation services while Shibboleth transmits attributes about users securely from the authenticating organisation so each content provider can individually decide whether to grant access. In other words, Athens centralises account administration and access to resources while Shibboleth relies on a federated architecture which distributes responsibility for managing user accounts and access across organisations and service providers. Aside from their differences in scope and architecture, Athens is a commercial service whereas Shibboleth is an open standard.

Integrated identity management challenges

Though LDAP can be an elegant solution for many digital library applications, sometimes no authentication or identity management application mechanism is supported by all library services. When this occurs, integrated authentication is only possible if patron data can be copied from one service to another, or if systems are configured to support multiple authentication methods. Under normal circumstances, this requires modest programming and data manipulation skills.

The Oregon State Library uses a central database to populate the patron databases used by the ILS, interlibrary loan system, legislation tracking and other services provided by the library. By storing all information in a widely available database management system, personnel and applications can easily read, modify and delete information in the database using standard utilities available on desktop machines and servers. The Oregon State Library uses this capability to automatically create and update patron data when patrons register for services or modify their username. As a result, patrons and staff do not have to modify information in multiple systems.

However, digital library integrators should give pause before developing systems that copy user information from one system to another. The systems to which data is copied may have their own native interfaces that allow their users to change data, which can lead to synchronisation problems. Various systems often support different conventions for usernames and passwords, including different encryption algorithms. Transferring data between systems may be difficult or impossible and risk compromising sensitive personal data. Furthermore, disabling accounts across multiple systems is inherently difficult.

The Web and digital library services are becoming increasingly personalised – this inherently requires libraries to track a certain amount of user activity. Effective personalisation requires web applications to retain preferences as users navigate across applications and web pages. At the same time, library management may require detailed statistics about how expensive resources are used to justify their continued funding. Lastly, some vendors may demand a mechanism that allows them to detect and disable users who abuse services. However, these goals must be accomplished without jeopardising the privacy or personal information of library users.

Session management and anonymous tokens are useful for tracking users as they use various web applications. They allow data about the user to be stored on the server rather than the less secure alternative of cookies on the computer workstation. When a person accesses a web page in an application that supports tokens, the application checks a cookie on the individual's machine that identifies the user with a token associated with a profile stored on the server. Web scripting languages, such as PHP support this type of session management and make it easy to create web applications that are smart enough to track user activity across web pages.

Single sign on (SSO) mechanisms, such as Athens allow users to log in at any one of several web applications (university portal, ILS, etc.) and be automatically logged into all others supported by the organisation. SSO is extremely useful for creating library portals as discussed in Chapter 9. SSO systems often utilise anonymous tokens for session management.

Data, network and server security

Most discussions about security focus on thwarting attacks, but the true purpose of network security work is to make hardware, services, programs and data as reliable as possible while preventing unauthorised use. Good security protects users against data loss caused by hardware failure and ensures that people do not gain inappropriate access to data or services. For example, libraries are legally obliged to make sure that they only grant access to research databases to those for whom the library has paid access. Libraries also are responsible for ensuring that data about patrons is kept secure.

Preventing, detecting and resolving security breaches require substantial resources and these costs must be balanced with library goals. Backing up data, monitoring system and network activity, checking hardware and performing other security activities consume significant technical and staff resources. Time and money devoted to security cannot be used to improve other library services, so dedicating excessive resources to security undermines library services.

Security is a serious concern for digital libraries. While this book largely focuses on web-based technologies that make up digital libraries, we will by necessity expand our scope when discussing security. Security for digital libraries does not stop at the web server or even the network operating system. The security of the entire network on which a digital library is mounted – including the network infrastructure and the personal computers and servers that are a part of it – is essential for sound digital library operations. Likewise, those supporting digital libraries cannot alleviate security concerns with a purely inward perspective. In many ways the Internet is still an untamed, lawless environment and most security concerns for digital libraries are Internet-wide issues. Digital library integrators must by necessity monitor security developments on the Internet that apply to the broad range of systems that they support.

On the surface, one would expect that libraries would not be interesting targets for attacks by hackers. Library personal computers and servers are usually not very powerful and the data that they contain would seem uninteresting. Libraries have few enemies. However, even lowly desktop computers directly or indirectly offer hackers things they really want – information, disk space, processing power, network bandwidth and a platform from which to launch attacks. Most organisations protect servers relatively well, but it is essential to protect personal computers as well. A compromised desktop, laptop, or even handheld machine can collect passwords, probe other machines for weaknesses, distribute files and perform other tasks that undermine security.

As is the case with all successful products and occupations, hacking has become big business. In the early 2000s organised crime discovered that significant money can be made by hacking machines. The method is conceptually very simple. Programmers in poor countries are paid to hack machines and install programs known as zombies on them. Zombies simply wait until they receive an instruction to flood a computer with information. A group of zombies, known as a botnet, can then be aimed at companies that heavily rely on their Internet presence for purposes of extortion or to shut them down. Botnets can be rented and they are a serious threat to Internet security. While no library is likely to be the target of a zombie attack, library machines are very useful for purposes of conducting this sort of coordinated attack on another site. A few hundred computers acting in unison can easily blast a powerful computer with a high-speed connection off the Internet (Gibson Research Corporation, 2005).

In addition, hackers are always looking for ways to distribute copyrighted music, videos, software or pornography. Any machine with a high-speed connection has plenty of drive space and processing power to distribute gigabytes of illegal or illicit materials. Hackers do not want to pay for the system resources necessary to distribute these types of materials – or to be held liable for breaking into systems, copyright infringement, sexual harassment, or distributing child pornography. For these reasons, library servers and even desktop machines are tempting targets.

Information is also a common target. If any device that remembers keystrokes is installed on a staff or patron computer (whether hardware or software, such as with a Trojan horse), a malicious user can easily obtain administrative passwords, financial data or patron information. Libraries that cling to the ill-advised practice of using social security numbers as patron identification numbers are particularly tempting targets for identity thieves.

Digital library integrators must also be aware of a variety of attacks that can be mounted against the web applications that they design themselves or purchase from others. For pre-packaged applications, they should be sure to stay on a recently updated, secure version. For home-grown applications, they should abide by secure coding practices and conduct periodic audits of applications running for security holes. Digital library integrators should seek out security best practices for the web scripting technology that they use.

Web application programmers should always validate whatever data a user submits to the application. A web application that does not check incoming data can be vulnerable to an 'SQL injection' attack, in which a malicious user sends a query to their database in order to view or modify data that they are not authorised to access.

Cross-site scripting attacks also rely on un-validated data. For example, many web-based programs (e.g. electronic bulletin boards, mailing lists, blog software, web collaboration tools, etc.) allow users to manually embed HTML code. If users are permitted to embed JavaScript in pages, a malicious user can execute a cross-side scripting attack that can potentially be used for identity theft. Cross-site scripting attacks (also known as XSS) use JavaScript to draw what looks like a legitimate web page that tricks users into revealing confidential information, automatically redirects them to a malicious site, or performs some other undesirable function (Zimmer, year unknown). XSS attacks represent no direct threat to the library server, but they definitely can harm library users.

How systems are compromised

Although people often focus on the actions of anonymous hackers when thinking about security, IT managers and systems administrators should be aware that research shows that the greatest permanent damage to systems and data results from errors and purposeful actions taken by staff and volunteers. As a result, good security requires reasonable precautions against damage by staff activity as well as unknown assailants on the Internet.

There are many methods and tools for breaking into systems, but most attacks are aimed at what are likely the weakest and most easily exploitable aspects of security – human users, well-known software bugs and machines with poor physical security. The easiest way to break into a system is to simply trick a victim into installing a virus or other malicious software onto their computer. Many computer users install programs without knowing anything about who created them or why. Games, screensavers, illicit materials and other types of popular software are often used to transport malicious software.

Successful computer viruses behave much like viruses in the regular world – the victim is typically not aware that a problem exists until they have already spread the disease to many others. If a malicious program causes immediate and obvious harm to a victim's computer, it is very easy to identify what caused the problem and keep it from propagating. On the other hand, if the malicious program performs a useful function and does not do anything that the victim recognises as harmful for weeks (or possibly ever), the victim themselves may help spread the malicious software by encouraging others to install it.

A significant percentage of attacks rely on well-known software bugs. For example, late on 24 January 2003, the Slammer worm crashed servers and congested or stopped Internet traffic worldwide for more than 9 hours by exploiting a weakness in Microsoft's SQL Server 2000 software. However, if systems administrators had installed a free patch that Microsoft had made available since July 2002, the attack would have had no effect. Likewise, the Netsky, Code Red and Nimda worms that affected hundreds of thousands of computers and caused billions of dollars in damages also exploited known weaknesses for which patches were available. No software is created perfect and many hackers use programs to search the Internet for computers running software with known vulnerabilities.

Attacks may employ multiple techniques at the same time. For example, a library volunteer might install a screensaver that probes the local network for known weaknesses or installs a Trojan horse that e-mails administrative passwords to the hacker. As new security mechanisms are developed, so are new methods of circumventing those mechanisms.

It is important to be aware that library staff, patrons or volunteers might attempt to gain inappropriate access to library systems and data, as well. It is far easier for identity thieves to get jobs where they have access to databases that contain personal information for thousands of people than it is for them to intercept and decipher communications on the Internet. Disgruntled present or former staff may also delete or modify data.

Tools to prevent security breaches

No tool or combination of tools can protect library machines and data from all attacks. However, an organisation armed with good computing practices, knowledge of how local systems behave and a few tools can be protected very effectively. These include automatic updating services, firewalls, antivirus software, alarms and encryption.

Security vulnerabilities on computer operating systems and software are continuously being discovered and published. The best strategy for keeping both servers and personal computers up-to-date and secure is to subscribe to an updating service that installs patches to software and operating systems automatically. These services are available for most commercial server and personal computer operating systems today. Although they do not work on specially compiled and customised applications, they are valuable for whatever standard software and operating systems that a library uses.

Firewalls

A hardware firewall is an essential first line of defence that can prevent or stop certain Internet based attacks on library networks by allowing network administrators to block certain types of connections and data transmissions. That said, the role of firewalls in ensuring security is often exaggerated. In practice, firewall management has tended to focus on port blocking, a simple and effective defence against attacks that require access to specific ports. However, malicious software writers have developed a wide variety of techniques to circumvent port blocking.

Software and hardware firewalls can allow libraries and their parent organisations to decide what type of networked applications can be run within their organisation. Such firewalls can be used to prevent users from sharing music, accessing online videos or other services. Libraries need to align these kinds of restrictions with the goals of their digital library services. For example, if a library filters nothing, it may find that its high speed connection gets overwhelmed by young patrons sharing music and games. Aside from creating potential legal problems, such a policy could effectively render the network unusable at certain times of the day. Likewise, a security policy that inadvertently prevents library users from accessing critical resources may do more harm than the attacks it is supposed to prevent.

Antivirus software, alarms and analysis tools

Reputable antivirus software can significantly reduce the chances of a system compromise on library servers and workstations, but it is not a substitute for observing safe computing practices. No antivirus software detects all viruses, and antivirus software that is not kept up-to-date is next to useless.

Alarms monitor networks and files monitor activity to alert systems administrators of unusual activity. Systems staff need to know who logs in from where, what changes are made to files, switches and other equipment, how much data is being transferred and a number of other indicators of systems activity. On most systems, there is far more activity than can reasonably be monitored by a human.

Hackers often do nothing for some time after they have gained access, so if their entry is not detected quickly, they can quietly obtain passwords, steal information and compromise backup files. Commercial alarm products are available, but systems administrators can easily design effective alarms and traps that alert them to unusual activity but that ignore routine work.

As a policy matter, staff and users should be notified that their actions may be monitored for maintenance purposes. Maintaining, protecting and troubleshooting systems necessarily requires the ability to detect and examine unusual activity. It is important to recognise that monitoring networks and machines for illegitimate activity is distinct from the kind of surveillance that compromises user privacy.

To troubleshoot problems and detect intrusions, it is necessary to monitor network activity. Many hardware and software tools exist, but a simple packet sniffer and a port-scanning tool can be extremely useful for detecting and resolving problems.[3] By identifying unusual patterns, such as machines communicating on suspicious ports or unusual levels of traffic, it is possible to identify many attempts to compromise machines, as well as ones that have already been hacked.

Encryption

Encryption prevents data from being monitored or altered. Generally speaking, any sensitive information transmitted over a local network or over the Web – financial information, passwords, forms that contain personal data, etc. – should be encrypted. In the digital library environment, data about library patrons is the main candidate for encryption. The intellectual content delivered over digital libraries may be copyrighted, but generally need not be encrypted because of the minimal potential for malicious use. Libraries should ascertain whether their web applications that exchange user data support encryption use the secure sockets layer (SSL) protocol. Typically, the library will need to purchase SSL certificates from a recognised certificate authority for all of the separate web servers (or virtual servers) that they use that support SSL authentication.

The practical value of encryption tends to be overstated. Encrypting data that does not need protection consumes substantial computing resources and has no practical effect aside from slowing system and network performance. Even when wireless connections that can easily be monitored by anyone are being used, one should remember that most sessions that need encryption are already secure. Financial sites, login screens to e-mail systems and a variety of other services already use encrypted sessions, so encrypting the encrypted stream again does not noticeably improve security. In addition, encryption provides no protection against Trojan horses or malicious websites because the former intercept the information before it is encrypted and the latter can interpret it after it is decrypted.

Basic systems and network protection

Following a few best practices can significantly improve network and server security.[4] Before implementing any specific security measure, systems administrators should consider whether the tools and methods are appropriate for local users and systems. Otherwise, critical work could be impeded or systems could be inadequately protected.

Most security policies are common sense. The following are security best practices that we recommend:

- Software, especially operating software and antivirus software should be kept up-to-date at all times using automated updating software if available.

- For key software that cannot be updated automatically, staff should join announcement lists that share news about any developments that concern the software.

- All valuable data should be backed up and stored in a separate physical location. At the very minimum, several weeks of data should be stored. Otherwise, if it takes a while to detect an intrusion, the backups may all be compromised as well.

- Personal and server computers should be physically secured to prevent devices, such as keystroke loggers, from being used.

- Administrators should take measures to prevent poorly chosen passwords and carelessly conceived group accounts.

- Administrative accounts that grant high access privileges to files on servers should not be used except when this is necessary to accomplish the task at hand.

- Encrypted connections should be used when logging into servers or applications, especially when doing so off-site.

- Systems staff should monitor access logs and write scripts that send alerts when unusual activity occurs.

- Lastly, systems administrators should remove or disable unneeded software or services as these increase the number of potential entry points to a system.

User behaviour is an important component of security. Staff and to some extent public users should be educated about these practices and the benefits of keeping systems secure.

Just as regular check-ups are a good idea for protecting one's health even when nothing seems wrong, good systems administrators routinely check systems for irregularities rather than wait for problems to emerge. Occasionally scanning raw log files, network activity, process lists, etc. can help systems personnel become intimately familiar with their systems so they can easily recognise anomalies and troubleshoot them quickly. Those who are charged with maintaining security should know what processes should be running, what ports should be open, how long it normally takes the machine to process routine operations and how much network activity they generate.

If systems are compromised

If systems are believed to be compromised, managers and systems personnel need to analyse the situation before taking action. It is very possible that the system in question was compromised days or even weeks before the intrusion was detected. If a server or a network is disabled the instant a problem is recognised, staff and users will be prevented from conducting legitimate activities. Security measures should not cause more problems than they prevent.

System logs should be checked and any files that were left behind or modified during the attack should be modified. It is desirable to contain and repair the damage as soon as possible, but this can only be done if systems personnel understand how the hackers gained access, what they learned and how much damage they did. Running names of clues uncovered during the initial investigation (such as names of mysterious files or processes) into a web search engine can help staff learn very quickly about how systems were compromised and the procedures to remedy the problem.

Once the scope of the loss and damage has been covered, a recovery plan must be developed. In some instances, this can be as simple as using an automated tool to remove and disinfect a few files. Other times, it will be necessary restore files from backup. If damage from the security breach cannot be readily identified and corrected, the machine attacked will likely need to be rebuilt with a fresh installation of the operating system.

Under normal circumstances, any compromised password must be disabled. That said, one technique that may be useful for understanding who broke in, how and why is to secure all data and plant interesting but false information to tempt the hacker (e.g. false financial or personal data).

Conclusions

The quality of digital library services and the amount of time and money it takes to provide those services depends heavily on how effectively libraries can provide an integrated authentication/authorisation mechanism and manage user information. Unless a library is willing to purchase all products from its ILS vendor, an external authentication method based on LDAP is the best choice for most environments. LDAP authentication can be implemented and maintained relatively cheaply, but the process of tying various library services into the LDAP server and integrating patron information may require moderate programming skills.

The best way to maintain security is to observe common-sense computing practices and to educate users. If software is up-to-date, users refrain from downloading or viewing questionable material or engaging in other risky practices, standard authentication measures are in place and systems activity is regularly monitored, problems will occur only rarely, if at all.

Summary

- Libraries typically use completely separate products to check out materials, request items via interlibrary loan, access databases, connect to a wireless network, use library workstations and perform a number of other functions.

- Integrated authentication is essential if people are going to use one username and password for all services.

- Most online library services have a built-in system for holding user data and performing authentication/authorisation, but these mechanisms usually cannot communicate with each other.

- There are many authentication methods, but most libraries are best served by relying on LDAP or ILS authentication.

- Automatically distributing patron information across different systems is difficult because each service needs different patron information.

- LDAP is not a panacea and levels of support for the standard vary. Libraries should check with vendors before assuming that a specific product can use LDAP as desired.

- Sometimes no authentication mechanism is supported by all library services. When this happens, custom programming is necessary.

- The primary goal of security is to ensure availability of services, not prevent attacks.

- Preventing, detecting and resolving security breaches require substantial resources; these costs must be balanced with library goals.

- Most damage to systems and data results from mistakes, bad training and purposeful actions taken by staff and volunteers – not hacker activity.

- No tool or combination of tools can protect library machines and data from all attacks. However, observing good computing practices and taking modest precautions can substantially increase security.

- Before implementing any specific security measure, systems administrators should consider whether or not the tools and methods are appropriate for local users and systems.

- User buy-in to security policies is absolutely critical, because users who engage in risky behaviour and circumvent security measures create weak points in the security chain that can be broken.

Notes

1 See *http://www.openldap.org/* (accessed: 17 February 2006).
2 See the Shibboleth Project site at: *http://shibboleth.internet2.edu/* (accessed: 17 February 2006).

3 See, for example: 'Snort – the de facto standard for intrusion detection/ prevention', *http://snort.org* (accessed: 17 February 2006); 'Nmap – free security scanner for network exploration & security audits', *http://www.insecure.org/nmap/* (accessed: 17 February 2006); 'TCPDUMP public repository', *http://www.tcpdump.org* (accessed: 17 February 2006).

4 See, for example: *http://www.winguides.com/security* (accessed: 17 February 2006) and *http://www.cert.org/security-improvement* (accessed: 17 February 2006).

5

Interfacing with integrated library systems

In the not so distant past, the integrated library system (ILS) was the overwhelming focus of technology endeavours in academic and public libraries. Today, ILSs remain the central piece of technology in most libraries. They are essential for the continued maintenance of a physical collection, especially in the areas of acquiring, cataloguing and circulation of that collection. They also provide library management with essential financial data on collection development expenditures and collection usage. Increasingly they play a role in managing a library's digital presence. This role can include software modules that support digital library activities, such as proxy servers, link resolvers and electronic resource management systems. The ILS can also be a storehouse of library specific data that can be accessed, manipulated and reused by other digital library applications.

Covered in this chapter:

- the current and future role of the ILS in digital library integration;

- accessing, manipulating and repurposing ILS data;

- connecting the ILS with other digital library systems;

The role of the ILS in the digital library

Like other management information systems, ILSs are typically a very large investment for a public or academic library. Often they require a substantial upfront purchase cost and also involve annual support and maintenance fees. It is not uncommon for this investment to be much more expensive than all of the other technology purchased by a library. Given that libraries are increasingly focusing on their digital presence, is the position of the ILS at the centre of library technology in question?

Several factors support the notion that the ILS will remain at the centre of library technology even as digital library management becomes a greater concern to libraries:

- Many ILS vendors have built a degree of trust with libraries. Libraries have grown to depend on their particular ILS vendor to provide them more-or-less reliable systems for maintaining their daily operations.

- Libraries have substantial investments in their ILS systems, both financially and in the personnel costs involved with learning those systems.

- Library staff are familiar with how ILSs work. They understand the record structures and workflows built into their ILS. Jerry Kline, president and CEO of Innovative Interfaces, has observed that carrying the 'same intellectual logic' from older ILS software into newer ILS software is important (Pace, 2004). Digital library tools offered by ILS vendors tend to employ the same workflow patterns, record structures and software interfaces as the central ILS product produced by the same company.

- ILS vendors are adapting to new circumstances and providing the tools needed to build digital libraries. A few of them are leading the way in digital library technologies.

There are, however, strong challenges to the integrated library system's position at the centre of library technology:

- Internet technologies have made it increasingly possible to distribute the kinds of systems and content that libraries need across separate software applications. The Web is a kind of common denominator platform that allows an organisation to deliver many separate applications to its user base through the web browser. Web services based APIs and emerging standards, such as SRU/W (Search and Retrieve via URL/Web service) and NCIP (NISO Circulation Interchange Protocol) will allow digital library components produced by separate vendors to interact with each other seamlessly.

- Library collection development now emphasises access over ownership. The ILS has historically served to manage purchased physical resources, but libraries are increasingly focusing their collection development efforts on providing to access to digital resources.

- Legacy technologies, such as MARC, as well as databases optimised for MARC records are heavily entrenched within ILS vendors' products. The familiar workflows and 'business logic' designed to work with MARC records and print materials may not effectively solve digital library problems.

- ILS vendors themselves are offering their products in forms decoupled from their central product and thereby breaking down a monolithic model of library technology. Examples abound of libraries running link resolvers, electronic resource management systems and digital collections systems from vendors other than their primary ILS vendor.

- ILS vendors may not compete well against smaller, more specialised and highly competitive firms using different business models. Companies, such as DiMeMa (CONTENTdm), Serials Solutions/ ProQuest (Article Linker OpenURL resolver) and Useful Utilities (EZproxy) are offering very effective and moderately priced digital library products. Firms like Serials Solutions are leveraging data as well as continuously updated, hosted software to compete with ILS vendors in digital library management applications. These companies are free to engineer their products without the constraints of legacy software. They often sell their software as an affordable service rather than as a large up-front purchase.

- Many of the technologies needed to build digital libraries are commodity technology that can be pieced together at relatively low cost. Not every library will have the expertise to do this, but the situation creates a low barrier to entry for firms that want to compete against traditional ILS vendors in the market for digital library solutions.

- Open source software options are available for many of the components that integrated library system vendors are marketing. These include digital collection management systems like DSpace, Greenstone and Fedora, as well as portal solutions, such as MyLibrary and the open source ILS, Koha.

- Often, digital library problems cannot be solved by 'plugging in' a prepackaged product. Solutions that are tailored to local environments require customised integration work that no ILS vendor can deliver.

The position of the ILS in the digital library is not likely to solidify anytime soon. It is instructive, however, to review the digital library products currently offered by ILS vendors and examine their relationship to the central ILS products of those vendors.

Digital library products offered by ILS vendors

In a blog post in early 2005, Lorcan Dempsey of OCLC asserts, 'it is clear that the ILS manages a progressively smaller part of library activity'. He goes on to outline the functions in a library that an ILS typically performs: acquisitions, cataloguing, circulation and the online public access catalogue (OPAC). He then lists functions not typically done by an ILS: resource sharing, metasearch/portal, resolver, electronic resource management/knowledgebase, portable bibliography, digital asset management (Dempsey, 2005).

Dempsey's observations ring true. Though integrated library system vendors are now offering many digital library products, a good portion of those products are decoupled from their main ILS product. Some libraries are choosing to solve the problems addressed by these products with home-grown software or products offered by non-ILS vendors. The phenomenon of non-ILS technology driving digital libraries is not new. In many ways, it began when libraries began creating their own web portals with home-grown HTML code in the 1990s.

The initial foray of ILS vendors into web-based digital libraries was the web OPAC, a natural extension of online catalogues that had been offered over Telnet connections or dumb terminals. The web OPAC has continued to evolve since its introduction in the mid-1990s. Innovations have included increased ability to customise display screens, relevance-based searching and enriched record content, such as book jacket images and table of contents data.

With the introduction of the web OPAC, ILS vendors introduced the ability to catalogue and link to resources on the Web. Many libraries took advantage of this feature by attempting to 'catalogue' portions of the Web, especially electronic journals and research databases. But the dynamic nature of the Web – the changing scope and location of content – proved challenging for ILS infrastructures designed to manage finite physical collections. Libraries found that their ILSs could not keep track of large sets of electronic journals provided by 'full-text' research databases. They began to go beyond static web pages and built web-based databases alongside their ILSs that allowed them to bulk-load electronic journal coverage data. They also found it necessary to configure their own remote access solutions that used CGI scripts or proxy servers to provide remote access to web-based subscription databases. It was not long before ILS vendors began offering their own prepackaged solutions to these problems.

In the late 1990s, ILS vendors began introducing products that provided authentication and proxying for remote users of electronic resources. These systems typically perform authentication against the ILS patron database before proxying a connection to a remote database. Often, they are substantially more expensive than low-cost proxy/authentication solutions like EZproxy, but provide added features, such as integration with ILS patron data and more refined usage statistics.

In the early 2000s, ILS vendors began work on electronic resource management (ERM) systems. The initiative to build ERM systems was stimulated in part by the Digital Library Federation's Electronic Resource Management Initiative, which established standards for records and workflow to build such systems (Jewell et al., 2004). ERM systems facilitate the management of electronic resources – from trial, to ordering and licensing, to ongoing use and renewal. When ERM systems are part of an ILS, they provide a method of tying the bibliographic data for things like electronic books and journals to the appropriate URLs and coverage data associated with those resources. They also allow for the frequent updating of volatile electronic journal coverage data, which can then coexist alongside more stable holdings data that tracks physical items in an ILS. Staff who are already familiar with their ILS workflow for book and serials acquisitions can often move into a similar workflow for processing electronic resources if their library has purchased their ILS vendor's ERM system.

Link resolvers are closely related to ERM products in that they also rely on electronic journal coverage data. The ILS vendor Ex Libris was the first major vendor to offer an OpenURL resolver product, 'SFX'. Ex Libris bought the beta version of the software used in the research and development process for the initial OpenURL standard and thereby positioned itself as the leader in OpenURL technology (van de Sompel, 2001). The case for purchasing a link resolver from the same vendor that provides a library's ILS is not as strong as it is in the case of an ERM system. Link resolvers do not typically involve an extensive staff workflow and will not benefit greatly from sharing the ILS staff interface. They can, however, benefit from integration with the ILS bibliographic and serials data as well as integration with an ILS OPAC. At least one ILS vendor only supports the display of their own link resolver in their web OPAC results.

Federated searching systems are another increasingly popular digital library product offered by ILS vendors. They create a single search interface to multiple online databases including OPACs, union catalogues, research databases, search engines, etc. A library purchasing a federated searching system from their ILS vendor can benefit from closer integration of ILS data in their federated search results as well as integration with their OPAC. Many ILS vendors rely on external firms, such as MuseGlobal for their federated searching technology. This reliance suggests that ILS vendors depend on customer relationships rather than technical prowess for the viability of these products.

ILS vendors have attempted inroads into the digital collections systems market by introducing digital collection management systems that run alongside the traditional ILS. By mounting a digital collection on the same platform as their ILS, a library will likely achieve better integration of metadata with their OPAC and enjoy familiar staff interfaces as they build their digital collection.

At least one ILS vendor is now offering a comprehensive portal product that will support the construction of a web gateway to all of a library's resources including 'the catalogue, databases, digital archives, RSS feeds, virtual reference, ILL, calendars, library news and general information and other library resources and services'. The product also supports subject specific gateways and federated searching (Sirsi Corporation, year unknown). Such a product essentially makes the library web page, perhaps the most common locally developed portion of a digital library, an ILS function.

Access to ILS data

With or without special digital library tools from their ILS vendor, there are currently many opportunities for libraries to better integrate their ILS into their digital library. Access to the data and functionality of the ILS are, however, often the limiting factor in this integration. The degree to which customers of an ILS vendor can access data can affect their ability to manipulate data in the ILS, connect the ILS to other important systems and repurpose the data in the ILS.

The most basic method of access to data in an ILS is via prepackaged public and staff interfaces designed for human interaction with the system. They are delivered using common platforms including Telnet, Windows, Java, and the Web. These interfaces are designed to promote efficient workflow in functional areas, such as cataloguing, serials management, circulation, acquisitions, etc. Using these interfaces, library staff enter data into the system as part of their workflow in each functional area.

Another common method of data access revolves around MARC loaders that allow the import and export of MARC records. A library might use these to export bibliographic records into a file, send them to a vendor for authority control processing and then reload them back into the system. Typically, this level of access is only available for bibliographic and in some cases, patron records. Order records, serial records, etc. can sometimes be automatically created along with bibliographic records loaded into the system, but it is less common to have the ability to export them and import them back into the ILS.

The ability to import and export records can be a powerful tool for database maintenance. It can also be a rather blunt instrument for making changes to an ILS database. Exporting, modifying and reloading records can be a time-consuming process and can interfere with real-time updating of those records while this process is being performed.

Another method of access to ILS data involves making direct connections to the underlying database on which the ILS runs. This tends to be possible when an ILS runs on a mainstream commercial relational database management system, such as Oracle. Depending on the way data is structured and the way permissions are granted, this allows programmers to read and modify the data in the ILS in real-time.

Figure 5.1 illustrates a web application connecting directly to the relational database that supports an ILS.

A further method of connecting to an ILS is through application programming interfaces (APIs), the specifications of which are published by the vendor of the ILS. APIs allow library staff to write their own applications that not only have the potential to interact with the data in the ILS, but also the software applications running on that ILS. When Duke University drafted a set of 'decision issues' for the selection of their integrated library system in 2003, they underscored the importance of APIs in a subsection entitled 'Potential for Local Customisation':

Figure 5.1 A web application connecting directly to the relational database that supports an ILS

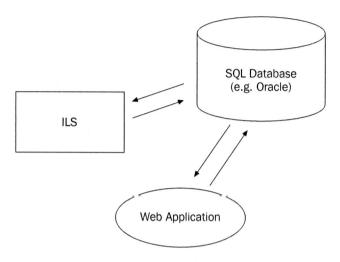

In a fast changing environment where users are aware of opportunities for significantly improved service and demand it, it is essential that the ILS vendor develop its product in an agile manner. It is highly desirable that ILS functionality lend itself to varied local implementation, so that the Duke libraries can tailor optimal services for their users to meet new and evolving needs. Access by library system staff to application programming interfaces (APIs) at an appropriate level of the data structure is a very strong indicator of the potential for customisation of the user interface, for the creation of specially tailored reports and for the integration of the ILS with other campus enterprise systems and with important library management systems. (Duke University Libraries, 2003)

At least one ILS vendor is now offering its APIs through more-or-less standards-based XML web services.[1] Because of the possibility for very flexible and platform independent interaction with the integrated library system, XML-based web services are one of the most promising and potentially useful methods of interaction with ILSs. To date, however, vendors offering such interfaces have only complied with web services standards, such as the Simple Object Access Protocol (SOAP) and library specific XML standards, such as MARC-XML, to varying degrees. One vendor offering an XML-based API to their web OPAC returns records in a non-standard XML format rather than the more-widely recognised MARC-XML format.

Figure 5.2 illustrates a web application accessing an ILS via a web services API.

If a library requires automated access to data in its ILS and direct database access and APIs are not available, they may resort to accessing ILS interfaces designed for human interaction in an automated fashion. This method of interaction generally takes the form of a script designed to simulate human interaction with a staff or public ILS interface. Expect scripts work well for accessing ILSs through Telnet or other command line interfaces. AutoIt scripts work with Windows based graphical user interfaces. If the data is available via a web interface, web scripting languages, such as PHP, can be used to connect to the website and extract desired data from the HTML pages returned. These 'back door' approaches are often referred to as 'hacks' or 'screen scraping'. Nonetheless, they provide a powerful tool for digital library integrators to overcome the barriers inherent in their ILS systems. Those using these techniques must beware of changes in the command line, windows or HTML interfaces with which their scripts interact. They also must be conscious of the inherent security risks of having computers masquerading as people.

Figure 5.2 A web application accessing an ILS via a web services API

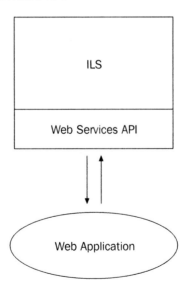

Manipulating the data in an ILS

The skills and technologies that libraries use to build digital library solutions are also important in maintaining integrated library system databases and tying them into a digital library environment. Due to the Internet and the availability of powerful data manipulation tools, libraries with skilled technologists can now perform sophisticated manipulation of the data in their ILS.

Catalogue librarians have performed database maintenance, including authority control and other global fixes and updates, ever since the inception of the ILS. Now, however, the data in ILSs no longer only applies to a relatively static physical collection of material. It can include hyperlinks to online sources and bibliographic records representing electronic journals, electronic books, local digital holdings and materials on order from online book vendors.

Because of the more fluid nature of the data within integrated library systems, advanced tools are needed to manipulate this data on an ongoing basis. Database preparation work, for which libraries paid firms to perform custom programming to manipulate their records, is no longer something that is only needed in rare cases, such as a system migration from one ILS to another. In order for a library to maintain a sound ILS database, it is almost mandatory that they have the staff expertise to perform advanced data manipulation across all record types in their ILS.

To freely manipulate the data in their systems, libraries need the ability to input and output records from their systems at will. They also need to the ability to modify those records using the conditional logic available in scripting/programming languages, preferably while the records are 'live' in the system. Simplistic global 'search and replace' features are not enough.

Here are a few scenarios in which sophisticated manipulation of the MARC records in an ILS (or destined to be loaded into an ILS) is useful:

- Thousands of URLs leading to electronic journals need to be modified according to a certain algorithm so that they conform to a new syntax of an electronic journal provider.

- Dublin Core Metadata from a digital collection system needs to be converted to MARC and loaded into an ILS.

- Provisional MARC records downloaded from a book vendor's website need to be modified so that they create order records with the proper codes when loaded into an ILS.

- MARC records for e-books need to be checked to see if they are relevant to a library's collection before adding them to the ILS database.

- A library needs to identify 50,000 books in its collection to be removed for space concerns based on a complex set of factors including age, subject addressed, date added to the collection, etc.

Tools, such as MarcEdit and the MARC::RECORD Perl package can be quite useful in performing tasks, such as those mentioned above (Highsmith, 2002; Reese, 2004). If an ILS allows for the flexible export and import of MARC records from an ILS, these programs allow almost unlimited flexibility in the automated examination and manipulation of records. MarcEdit only requires knowledge of the MARC record format to perform basic global editing functions. But to perform manipulation of records based on conditional logic in MarcEdit or MARC::RECORD Perl, one must have the ability to write scripts in Visual Basic or Perl.

An alternative approach to exporting records, modifying them and importing them back into an ILS is through direct interaction with the ILS database or through APIs. ILS systems that run on standard relational database management systems, such as Oracle may allow direct manipulation of data within those systems via SQL queries. This method of ILS data access requires skills in writing SQL queries or a program written specifically for your ILS vendor's database.

The Cataloger's Toolkit, a popular program designed for manipulation of MARC data in the Endeavor integrated library system uses this method of sending and receiving data from an ILS. According to its author, the Cataloger's Toolkit helps redress deficiencies inherent in the out-of-the box cataloguing client program. The Toolkit offers special functions that aid in authority control work, call number generation and batch corrections, among other things (Northwestern University Library, 2002).

When direct database access and APIs are not available, automated access to staff and public interfaces with languages, such as Expect and AutoIT are another option. Any number of functions on an ILS with a command line interface can be automated through Expect including:

- a repetitive task, such as moving data from order records to item records;

- the initialisation and verification of a backup tape on a daily basis;

- the extraction of data from the ILS database on a weekly basis for an external web application.

Connecting the ILS to other systems

Given that ILSs are an important reality in modern public and academic libraries, how should they be integrated into a broader Internet and digital library infrastructure? Connecting an ILS to other systems can be hard. ILSs are often designed as proprietary 'islands' of technology with very restricted communication channels to the outside world. Often there are very few 'hooks' available to outside applications that need to communicate with the ILS or simply extract data from it.

Libraries that purchase digital library components, such as link resolvers, electronic resource management systems, proxy servers, etc. from vendors other than their ILS vendor may experience challenges in connecting the systems together. Link resolvers and electronic resource management systems often need access to metadata and holdings data about print and electronic journals in the ILS. Libraries often achieve this data transfer through batch export of data from their ILS on a regular basis.

Linking in and out of a library's OPAC is a simple, lightweight technique for connecting the ILS to external digital library applications. Link resolvers that point users to print versions of library resources often link into an OPAC to show detailed holdings and status data. Libraries frequently link from their web portals to their OPAC when making reference to print or electronic works catalogued in their ILS. A common use for outbound links from a web OPAC is to link to electronic reserves from bibliographic records. If library staff have the ability to create outbound URLs (MARC 856 fields) in their ILS bibliographic records, they can create a simple electronic reserves system by mounting PDF documents on an authenticated external web server and cataloguing those documents in their ILS.

ILS patron data includes generic personal data, such as name, address, phone number and ID, as well as ILS specific data, such as materials checked out, overdue notices, etc. Importing and exporting patron data is an evolving area of interaction between the ILS and other systems. In the case of public libraries, the ILS is often the central repository of library patron data. If the library runs digital library applications like a proxy server or a separate interlibrary loan borrowing system, those systems need to have access to the patron data in the ILS in order to authenticate patrons and utilise common personal data like address and phone number.

In the case of academic libraries, the central source of patron data is often housed in a university-wide management information system that tracks students and employees. The integrated library system needs that data in an up-to-date form so that it can determine who is eligible for library services. The data often provides a number, such as a student ID to be used as a password to access personalised functions of the ILS, such as book renewals.

The most common means of exchanging patron data is by loading or exporting a file of it in delimited text or a MARC format into or out of the ILS. Although this method of exchanging data can be automated to occur weekly or even daily, it does not provide for real-time updating of patron information across systems and cannot be used to support a single username/password configuration across computing systems on a college/university campus.

A more advanced solution to patron authentication that allows for a single campus username/password employs LDAP. College and university IT departments commonly run an LDAP server populated with the latest student and employee data, including passwords. ILSs that are LDAP-aware allow patrons to log into the ILS with a username and password that is checked in real-time against an LDAP server, rather than fields in their database.

ILSs are also beginning to support 'single sign on' (SSO) in college/ university environments. SSO allows students to log in once to one of any number of university web applications (such as a course schedule, a grade reporting system, or course management systems) and be automatically logged into the other web applications. Innovative Interfaces introduced an SSO product that uses an Apache web server module to communicate with other web applications participating in SSO (Innovative Interfaces Inc., 2005).

Many colleges and universities run campus-wide 'portal' software that is designed to allow students a single point of access to their online experience at the institution. One ILS vendor now supports the ability to integrate with the open source uPortal project using 'channel' technology (Breeding, 2005). Plymouth State University has utilised local programming to integrate ILS functionality, such as book renewals and proxying to their off-campus databases into their campus wide portal. They achieve the integration not through APIs or standards-based interfaces, but by 'lots of local programming' in PHP which simulates a patron logging into the ILS in the background (Allard and Bisson, 2004). Hamilton College also uses PHP to extract data including overdues, fines, requests and course reserves, from the patron web interface to their OPAC and put it into their campus portal system (Herold, 2004).

Better integration between ILSs and external systems could bring many improvements to library services. For example, an external interlibrary loan (ILL) system, such as OCLC's ILLiad or Clio Software's Clio that could communicate circulation transactions to an ILS would allow a library patron's ILL materials to be tracked from their ILS record. To achieve such integration, ILS vendors will need to publish their APIs and, when possible, make the functionality of their systems available through standards-based protocols, such as NCIP.

RSS feeds driven by an ILS OPAC promote interconnection between ILSs and external systems. Sirsi offers a product that allows library patrons to create an RSS feed for any search done through their OPAC (Sirsi Corporation, year unknown). The Seattle Public Library has developed external scripts that create secure RSS feeds that show what books a particular patron has checked out, has on hold, etc. Using the system, patrons can show off their reading lists on their blogs (Malhotra, 2005). In general, RSS feed technology is useful for integration challenges, such as bringing electronic reserve readings into course management systems and importing library circulation data into campus portals.

Repurposing ILS data

Data within an ILS can often be repurposed in external web applications that offer functionality not possible with the software provided by an integrated library system. Some examples of such web applications are:

- a journal title search that includes print journals catalogued in the ILS and electronic journals provided by electronic journal aggregators;

- portal management software, such as MyLibrary, that allows librarians and patrons to organise resources in their personal web portal, including resources catalogued in the ILS;

- a web application that allows browsing the bibliographic content of the ILS by subject;

- a system that displays recent library acquisitions in particular subject areas and produces RSS feeds of those acquisitions.

There are two popular methods of constructing such systems. The first utilises an API or direct database query to the ILS data. This method allows one to avoid building an intermediary database and instead accesses the data in the ILS in real-time. Arkansas Tech University uses PHP scripts to extract data from the Oracle database that supports their Endeavor ILS. By querying the database in real-time with PHP, they can produce specialised web reports for multimedia materials, room scheduling and recent acquisitions.[2] Even when using the direct database access/ API approach, construction of a secondary database is sometimes necessary so as to optimise the database structure for the queries that the external application performs.

The other method of constructing such a system involves exporting data from the ILS and storing it in an external relational database, such as MySQL or PostgreSQL. Exporting the data on a regular basis typically involves running scheduled scripts (such as Expect and PHP scripts) to achieve the export and database load. A web application development platform, such as PHP, Cold Fusion, or ASP can then be used to build the web application that queries the database and provides the web interface to the user.

Some libraries make special efforts to keep the ILS at the centre of their operation by recording all the local data that supports their digital library within their ILS. Often they utilise special fields in the MARC record to hold data (like non-standard subject headings or categories of authorised users) that are needed by their digital library applications. Such an approach allows staff to use the familiar interfaces of the ILS to enter and update data, and retains the status of the ILS as the database of record. Hong Kong University relies on data in its ILS to populate 'downstream' digital library applications, such as browsable web pages of electronic resources, a MyLibrary installation, an EZproxy installation, an online thesis database and an online table of contents database (Kammin and Palmer, 2004).

ILS case study at Lewis & Clark College

Lewis & Clark College's Watzek Library has developed three applications that leverage the data in their ILS for new purposes. The first is an extension to their integrated library system that allows patrons to browse their audiovisual collection in ways not permitted by their ILS OPAC.[3]

The audiovisual collection at Lewis & Clark is richly catalogued within the ILS bibliographic database. The library's cataloguers have added genre headings for its CDs derived from the musical genres and subgenres in the All Music Guide. Examples of these genres include: 'jazz', 'blues', 'country' and 'rock'; examples of subgenres include 'slide guitar blues', 'classic jazz', 'alternative country' and 'punk'. They have also added genre headings for videos derived from the genres in the Internet Movie Database, which includes a less extensive list of 20 or so film genres, such as 'film noir', 'science fiction', 'comedy', etc.

Although all of the content in the audiovisual database may be accessed through the search functionality of the library's OPAC, library patrons would have to employ fairly sophisticated search strategies to take advantage of the genre headings in the system. They would need to know the correct term for the genre ahead of time, as well as how to limit their search to the media that they seek.

The audiovisual browsing system allows patrons to browse the collection by language, format and genre using a simplified interface. Using pull-down menus, patrons may perform searches, such as: all DVDs in French, all videos and DVDs in German in the genre 'romance', all CDs in the genre 'country', etc. The system also effectively 'pre-packages' searches for musical subgenres ('slide guitar blues', 'hard bop', 'vocal jazz', 'film noir' etc.) that a user might not know off the top of their head when searching the traditional library catalogue.

The audiovisual database depends on the following scripts and processes developed locally by library staff:

- Once a week an Expect script connects to the ILS and creates a list of all bibliographic records for audiovisual titles.

- The Expect script instructs the ILS to create a comma separated values (CSV) file with the appropriate bibliographic (author, title, genre) and format (CD, record, DVD, video) data in it and uploads that file to the library's web server.

- A 'command-line' PHP script on the library's web server inserts the data from the CSV file into a PostgreSQL database running on that web server.

- A PHP script allows patrons to browse the database from the Web.

- When patrons find a title of interest, a link takes them directly to a full bibliographic display of the title (with circulation status information) in the ILS supported web OPAC.

Figure 5.3 illustrates the technical configuration behind Watzek Library's audiovisual database. An Expect script regularly populates an external SQL database that can be directly accessed by the web application.

Figure 5.3   Repurposing ILS data via Expect

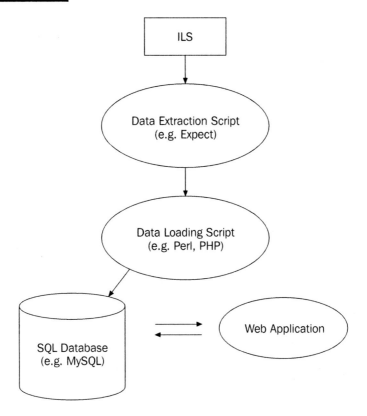

In many ways, the audiovisual database is simply a gateway to data kept within the ILS. The above process begins by exporting from the ILS and ends up returning to the ILS with a link back to a record in the ILS' OPAC. The audiovisual database assists the patron in finding the material that they are looking for in ways that the OPAC cannot achieve. But the ILS still contains the master data about the material, the circulation status of each item, as well as the capability to circulate the item. The system supplements the ILS in the area of searching but inventory control remains entirely within the ILS.

Watzek Library has built upon this database of audiovisual material and constructed an audio electronic reserves system. Using the bibliographic data in the audiovisual database as a foundation, the audio reserves system uses PHP scripts to support management of mp3 files created from CDs in the audio collection. The system allows students to access the music on CDs that are on reserve via a secure interface that organises the mp3s according to course and CD. The system relieves demands on CDs that music instructors place on reserve for their courses.

Watzek Library now also supports a 'new additions' database of books and other materials recently added to its collection. The database is populated using an Expect/PHP system similar to the one supporting the audiovisual database. Like the audiovisual database, it offers patrons a way of viewing ILS data that is not possible in the OPAC. Patrons can browse new additions by several subject headings derived from the classification numbers of the records in the database. They can also subscribe to RSS feeds that keep them informed of new additions in a particular subject area.

These systems demonstrate how libraries can use generic Internet technologies and custom programming to leverage the data in their ILS. They underscore the continued importance of the ILS in the management of a library collection while simultaneously revealing the limitations of the ILS in the realm of information discovery.

The future role of the ILS

It remains impossible to predict the future role of the ILS in the digital library. But we can speculate on a few different scenarios. Some observers foresee a 'dis-integrating' of the ILS. In one sense, 'dis-integration' could take the form of ILS vendors using more mainstream software components, such as external databases, search engine software and other pre-designed business-logic software to build their systems. On a 2005 oss4lib discussion list post, Art Rhyno makes the case for a more component-based ILS. He observes that other industries take advantage of generic software components more so than ILS vendors, who have only recently moved from their own proprietary databases to common commercial database systems:

> What if the bright minds behind the vendor solutions could concentrate on the unique parts of library systems rather than architecting transaction support and other functions that are already out there? My guess is that changing or upgrading an ILS would be less like adopting a monolithic monster from a small family that doesn't get out much, which seems to be what happens now. Still, there was a time when using a relational database behind an ILS was considered a pretty radical step, I don't think any serious

library vendor would now argue that building their own database system is a particularly good idea, at least for a large organisation, so maybe we are making some progress after all. The difficulty is that user expectations are so high now that spending too much time perpetuating the ILS' primary function as an inventory control system detracts from what needs to happen to make the public side more compelling (Rhyno, 2003b).

Dis-integration could also take the form of dividing the ILS into several components that communicate with each other using standards-based APIs. As Andrew Pace puts it:

> Library vendors have two choices. They can continue to maintain large systems that use proprietary methods of interoperability and promise tight integration of services for their customers. Or, they can choose to dismantle their modules in such a way that librarians can reintegrate their systems through web services and standards, combining new with the old modules as well as the new with each other. (Pace, 2004).

A further dis-integration scenario would be a renewed divide between the searching and the inventory control functions of ILSs. ILSs are particularly good at managing library assets. Traditionally these have been physical assets but increasingly ILSs are also managing digital assets through ERM systems. ILSs can track these assets throughout their lifecycle from initial consideration to ordering to usage. The ILS works well as an 'inventory control system'.

But ILSs are much weaker when it comes to the discovery of the intellectual content of the collections that they manage. Admittedly, many ILSs now have the capability of enriching bibliographic records with table of contents data as well as cover art. But for the most part, the bibliographic records that OPACs search are limited in descriptive quality and not connected to any dynamic mechanisms that keep them up-to-date.

ILS OPAC search functionality is far inferior to web search engines like Google. Most OPACs have non-standard methods for nesting, phrase-searching, truncation, stop words and wildcarding. Their relevance ranking capabilities tend to be weak compared with search engines. There is often limited inclusion of and linking to relevant material (Pace, 2005). The popularity of search engine style searching has continued to draw attention to the deficiencies of the Boolean 'keyword' searching available in most ILS OPACs. A study published in 2004 indicates that users of library OPACs are regularly attempting to use search engine style searching in web OPACs, often with poor results (Yu, 2004).

The following initiatives have further demonstrated the limitations of the OPAC as we know it: Google Book Search, in which the full text of books is searchable; Open WorldCat, in which library holdings appear in search engine results that refer to books (OCLC, year unknown); and RedLightGreen (*http://www.redlightgreen.com*), a search engine for books that uses the number of libraries holding the books as one of its measures of relevancy.

A report from University of California Libraries (2005), 'Rethinking How We Provide Bibliographic Services for the University of California' recommends significant changes to the systems that search the bibliographic content of the university's library catalogues. It proposes consolidating the library catalogues to a single database so that all updates to catalogue records could be shared. A single database, the report adds, would ease the creation of discovery and presentation services that lay atop the data store. The report recognises that with a single catalogue, the library system would be able to leverage economies of scale to provide the best information discovery technologies available. The report recommends looking beyond ILS vendors for the development of such a catalogue and mentions OCLC, Google or RLG as possible organisations that could develop and support it.

In 2006 North Carolina State University (NSCU) unveiled a new web OPAC that utilises technology independent from their ILS vendor. It is based on the Endeca ProFind platform, a search system that has been used by large corporations to enhance searching of their public websites and intranets. The new OPAC takes advantage of classification numbers and subject headings as well as format and genre data in the library's ILS to create an extremely flexible way of searching and browsing the entire library collection. Patrons performing a keyword search receive relevance ranked results. They also receive a view of the most common subject headings, formats and genres that their search has retrieved and the number of results within those categories.[4]

If other libraries follow NCSU's lead, we might see a future scenario where content browsing, searching and linking become decoupled from ILS functions like circulation, ordering and electronic resource management. In a return to its origins, the ILS might be relegated to 'back-room' operations, while external systems take over the searching duties (Borgman, 1997).

On the other hand, integrated library systems could regain their position at the centre of library technology as their digital library products mature. If the toolset of technologies required to run a digital library stabilises, the market for those technologies might consolidate down to a few vendors who sell digital library components in tightly integrated packages. Eventually, the ILS could evolve into a comprehensive content management system for digital libraries. A mix of current and new ILS vendors might build these systems, which, thanks to standards, would interface with information providers to create integrated digital library portals. Rather than attempt to manage all digital library data locally, they would be equipped with the tools to harvest, link to and search the local and remote resources that comprise a comprehensive digital library.

Summary

- A relationship of trust between ILS vendors and libraries, substantial investment by libraries in their ILS systems, library familiarity with the business logic of ILS systems and adaptation of ILS vendors to digital library needs are all factors that argue in favour of the continued centrality of the ILS in library technology.

- The low cost, flexibility and modularity of Internet technologies and new library standards, the trend of access over ownership, the rigid nature of legacy ILS systems, the modular nature of the digital library product market even among ILS vendors, the entry of non-ILS firms into the digital library technology market, the ubiquity of low-cost Internet technology, the availability of open source digital library tools and the customised requirements of many digital libraries are factors that argue against the continued centrality of the ILS in library technology.

- Since the dawn of the Web in the early 1990s, ILS vendors have been offering progressively more digital library products including web OPACs, proxy servers, electronic resource management systems, link resolvers, federated searching systems and digital asset management systems.

- There are four major strategies for accessing data in an ILS: human user interfaces, MARC loaders, direct database connections and APIs. Direct database connections and APIs offer the most flexibility, but for libraries whose ILSs do not offer these options, scripting languages, such as Expect, can facilitate automated access to data through interfaces designed for human interaction.

- Given the fluid nature of digital library data in an ILS, sophisticated tools for manipulation of ILS data are essential. MARC record manipulation tools, direct database access and scripting languages are all strategies that can accomplish such manipulation.

- Connecting the ILS to other systems, such as link resolvers, interlibrary loan systems, university management systems and university portals is often difficult due to the closed nature of ILS systems. APIs and standards like LDAP provide the ideal channel for integrating systems but creative 'hacks' are necessary in some cases.

- ILS data may be repurposed in external web applications that leverage web scripting languages and relational databases.

- Lewis & Clark College's Watzek Library has constructed three external applications that rely on data extracted from its ILS: an audiovisual browsing database, an audio electronic reserves system and a new books database. These systems supplement the searching functionality in the library's ILS OPAC.

- Common standards may allow the ILS to be more component-based in the future. The OPAC is an area of ILS functionality that could be replaced with systems external to the ILS, such as advanced search engines. Some larger libraries have already started to move in this direction.

Notes

1. See: *http://www.exlibris.co.il/aleph_architecture.htm* (accessed: 26 July 2005).
2. See (Calhoun 2005), available from the author.
3. To view these applications, visit the Aubry R. Watzek Library website: *http://library.lclark.edu* (accessed: 26 February 2006).
4. See NCSU (2006) and *http://endeca.com/solutions/enterprise_search.html* (accessed: 19 January 2006).

6

Electronic resource management

Licensed electronic resources consume a significant portion of library acquisition budgets, indeed most of the acquisition budget at many institutions. Managing digital subscriptions has naturally become a significant problem for libraries. Solutions have developed rapidly in recent years, with vendor and open source products ranging from integrated library system modules to hosted web applications. The strengths and weaknesses of these approaches merit scrutiny. An overall solution must facilitate both complex back-end tasks such as ordering and licence management in addition to front-end information discovery and access by library users. The goal of connecting back-end management solutions and front-end public services is a key challenge for digital library integration.

Covered in this chapter:

- the nature and origin of electronic resource management;

- functional overview of electronic resource management systems;

- specific management tasks and related standards;

- the advantages and limitations of various systems;

- a case study.

Emergence of electronic resources management

Managing print materials has lead to many of the characteristic organisational traits that we see in libraries today. Acquiring, cataloguing and circulating books and other print materials are distinct but interdependent activities carried out by separate units within the organisation. Traditional integrated library systems (ILSs) automate the work of these units, facilitating the labour-intensive workflows of traditional library operations, including the acquisition of materials for the physical collection and the maintenance of relatively permanent MARC records. Because licence arrangements between libraries and publishers rarely intrude on the use of books, journals and other offline content, such agreements fall outside the purview of a traditional ILS.

With the transition to web-based digital content, libraries confront new business and legal realities. Rather than acquire and manage permanent copies of individual titles, libraries increasingly buy *access* to digital content that has been bundled into aggregated packages. The content of these packages is often largely or entirely determined by the publisher and is subject to periodic or frequent change. Digital library collections are therefore more dynamic than print collections.

Licence contracts between publishers and libraries furthermore define terms of use, including who has access to a digital resource. Tracking and meeting licence terms introduces new requirements for resource management and the administration of library services.

The new management challenges, commonly grouped together under the heading of electronic resource management (ERM), thus include:

- evaluation, purchase and cancellation of digital content;

- management and tracking of licences and terms of use;

- discovery of and access to these resources.

Although ERM can be discussed as a subset of digital asset management (DAM), the topic of Chapter 7, it is best to think of these as two distinct activities. DAM focuses on digital content generated and owned by the library or parent institution, and on roles that reach beyond the traditional framework of library service. ERM, by contrast, focuses on the management of licensed digital content and tends, for now, to fit within the service framework traditionally offered by libraries.

We should note, however, that vendor product literature tends to use the term ERM in a more limited way than we do in this book. Vendors typically use the ERM label for software modules that support product evaluation and licence management. Yet these so-called ERM solutions achieve their full potential only when combined with other services, often sold separately.

From a software point of view, ERM is therefore best viewed as a combined strategy, one that integrates such tools as an OpenURL resolver, a licence management package, an acquisitions module and other tools provided by a single vendor or a combination of vendors, open source initiatives, or in-house development projects. Integrating licensed content into a digital library (Chapter 8), representing this content in existing library systems and web OPACs (Chapter 5), and providing user-centred web interfaces for diverse content streams (Chapter 9) are essential aspects of a complete ERM solution. Techniques for authentication and rights management (Chapter 4) are necessary to meet the terms of licence agreements. Library-specific information standards (Chapter 3) and cross-industry standards help facilitate access to licensed content.

ERM tasks

Although the stakes are highest at large institutions with multiple library branches and dispersed selection processes, ERM has significant implications for any library. It has been suggested that digital publishing trends will eventually 'eliminate much of what remains of the collection-development process and ... shift the librarian's role much more toward managing licenses' (Campbell, 2006). Whether or not this will someday be true of monographs, it is arguably already true of journal subscriptions.

Recognising this trend, librarians and library system vendors have spurred on the development of electronic resource management systems (ERMS). A key to achieving comprehensive ERM solutions is interoperability between a wide range of content management and access services, from A–Z journal lists to content acquisition and licence renewal. How well ERM systems achieve this integration is the chief concern of digital library integrators.

ERM potentially deals with many types of digital content. The most commonly discussed ERM challenge, however, is the management of electronic journal subscriptions, and managing this content will concern much of the discussion to follow. Other common types of licensed digital content include art images licensed for local use and stored within a DAM service, digitised primary source material hosted off-site and electronic books and reference sources. ERM management solutions apply to all types of licensed digital content regardless of publication type or media.

ERM activity might therefore be called the 'brains' behind well-managed digital library services. To see the full range of what an ERMS might do, it helps to think in terms of an electronic resource lifecycle composed of discovery, trial, selection, acquisition, access and renewal or cancellation. The Holy Grail of ERM is management of this entire lifecycle, with support for the following kinds of tasks:

- discovery of new products;

- product evaluation and comparisons;

- licence negotiation;

- ordering and renewal;

- tracking licence terms;

- point of use information about licence terms and technical support;

- creation of web gateways;

- individual title access through catalogues, searchable title lists and link resolvers;

- overlap analysis of database products;

- usage analysis;

- access management;

- proxy services.

Because these tasks span different units of the library, integrated ERM solutions promise increased efficiency by eliminating redundant management steps.

Because ERM involves so many library functions, existing integrated library systems (ILSs) appear positioned to play a central role. Yet for reasons outlined at the outset of this chapter, ILS vendors have been in a game of catch-up. As noted in the report of the Digital Library Federation's Electronic Resource Management Initiative:

As libraries have worked to incorporate electronic resources into their collections, services and operations, most of them have found that their existing integrated library systems (ILSs) are not capable of supporting these new resources. (Jewell et al., 2004)

As a consequence, some of the earliest ERM solutions were developed in-house and dealt with specific aspects of the ERM problem. Some of these local solutions were ambitious, others more modest.

Commercial services also carved out a new market for partial ERM solutions, introducing products that are now widely used in the library community. Two leading examples are Serials Solutions (ProQuest), whose original product was HTML formatted lists of electronic journal coverage data and SFX, a pioneering OpenURL product from Ex Libris that, like most link resolver solutions, provides a knowledgebase of coverage data for licensed content. Both of these services addressed the problem of access to full-text journal articles.

Early entrants into the ERM marketplace are today aggressively expanding the range of products that they offer. And they face stiff competition now that the ERM problem is widely recognised. An April 2005 guide to ERM systems in *Serials Review* discussed 11 licence management systems offered by different vendor types, each of which suggests a unique route to integration with other digital library services (Collins, 2005). This forces digital library integrators and library management to consider a number of possibly competing realities when making ERM decisions. ERM solutions offered by vendors must be evaluated within the broader context of the library or parent organisation's goals for digital library services and content integration.

ERM functional overview

The functional requirements of an ERM solution are roughly divided between front-end discovery and access services and back-end staff functions. Front-end services address the needs of end-users and contribute significantly to the library's public service profile. These services include link resolvers, proxy servers, A–Z lists and other access services. Back-end functions include the tracking of licence terms, monitoring renewal dates and fund accounting.

Figure 6.1 is a simplified model that illustrates some of the components of a comprehensive ERM solution. Three primary capabilities are illustrated:

- The *business transactions* component is ideally used by all library acquisitions activities, regardless of material type. Business transactions will typically be handled by the acquisitions module of an integrated

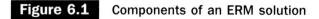

Figure 6.1 Components of an ERM solution

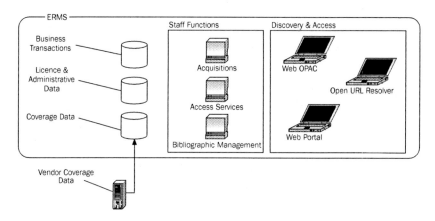

library system. A library could conceivably use different business tools for different material types.

- The *licence and administrative data* component allows a library to track both terms of licence agreements and other details related to managing and using an online resources, including administrative passwords. Licence and administrative information will typically be entered manually by qualified staff.

- The *coverage data* component is a largely automated service capable of ingesting normalised data from vendor title lists or publication access management services (described in the following section). Coverage data might also be harvested from local sources, like an ILS or a repository. It should be possible to enter data manually when necessary. Coverage data must be shared by a number of different ERM services.

Figure 6.1 illustrates three primary staff functions associated with these core ERM components. *Acquisitions* refers to a wide range of activities, from identifying and evaluating new products to licence negotiation and purchase. *Access services* include such activities as managing proxy servers and web portals, troubleshooting problems at a public service desk, or fulfilling interlibrary loan requests using licensed digital content. *Bibliographic management* involves managing and updating coverage data.

Discovery and access tools utilise information from each of the main functional components of an ERM solution. Coverage data is made available to users through web OPACs, OpenURL resolvers, or web portal services and is optionally augmented with licence and administrative information at the point of need (for example, usage restrictions tracked by an ERM licence module can be available to users of the library's web portal). The current state of subscriptions as tracked with ERM acquisition modules might be seamlessly reflected in the public access paths to digital content.

The range of ERM needs illustrated in Figure 6.1 could theoretically be addressed through the purchase of complementary modules from a library's ILS vendor. All digital library services would thus be integrated within a more or less closed library system. A number of ILS vendors appear to be focused on this path to the future. An alternative path utilises web services and open APIs (described in Chapter 5) to support a mix of ILS modules, third-party applications and locally developed web applications combined as needed in a comprehensive ERM solution. A third approach – one that might make sense in many library settings – divides the ERM problem into discrete parts and determines an optimal mix of partial solutions that meet a library's needs. This approach allows the library to pursue more comprehensive ERM strategies in realistic and incremental steps.

Libraries thus face significant choices. Before considering ERMS vendor solutions, it may be helpful to consider some defining aspects of ERM in greater detail.

Coverage data

There is a terminological problem that we need to address immediately in this section. Throughout this book, we use the term 'coverage data' to describe the information that OpenURL resolvers and other services use to provide access to a library's online journal subscriptions. The resources managed by an ERMS are not limited to serials publications, however. An ERMS thus needs to manage both non-serial and serial publications.

Electronic serials coverage data is nevertheless a central concern for ERM. In a traditional library setting, serials management involves tracking the receipt of journal issues and processing these issues as they are added to the library collection. Once a journal issue is received, recorded and placed on the shelf, the problem of access has been effectively solved. Bibliographic management of print materials thus relies on labour-intensive manual techniques that assume stability and slow, incremental growth.

Electronic journal publishing introduces requirements for bibliographic management that are difficult if not impossible to address using manual methods alone. Consider the external players and services involved in providing access and coverage data for electronic resources:

- publication hosting services, like Ingenta and HighWire Press, that offer electronic hosting services to publishers and, in turn, to journal subscribers;

- aggregation services, like ProQuest and EBSCOHost, that provide access to articles drawn from thousands of journal publications that are not managed or individually chosen by the library;

- collection publishers, like JSTOR and the American Chemical Society, that provide relatively stable journal collections, and, in the case of JSTOR, a permanent repository;

- publication access management services, like Serials Solutions and TDNet, that track the offerings of aggregation services, publication hosting services and electronic publishers;

- OpenURL linking services, like SFX and Serials Solutions, that gather and normalise holdings information from a variety of sources and provide appropriate copy access to library users.

Because access to electronic resources requires an on ongoing exchange of information between libraries and these partners, ERM solutions must be able to share data gracefully and with a minimum of manual intervention. For example, an aggregator like EBSCOHost provides journal coverage based on contracts with hundreds of publishers. When a library drops or adds an aggregator product like EBSCOHost, thousands of titles are immediately affected. In addition, because coverage within aggregations changes continuously, libraries must regularly download information from the vendor and incorporate this new coverage data into an ERMS, ILS or coverage database. Many, if not most, libraries rely on publication access management services like Serials Solutions or TDNet to do the work of gathering and normalising coverage data from vendors.

The need for publication access management services (PAMS) arguably arises from the lack of uniform standards for exchanging coverage data between players in the electronic journal marketplace. If widespread standardisation of coverage data is achieved, the need for PAMS will be mitigated, although PAMS may continue to offer enriched coverage data and leverage their extensive knowledgebase into other ERM products like link resolvers, MARC records, and enriched subject classification.

As standards go, the prospects for achieving consensus appear reasonably good in the case of coverage data. Coverage data for serials is, after all, relatively simple. It typically includes:

- publisher/hosting service;
- title;
- ISSN;
- start date;
- end date;
- base URL.

With the support or participation of most major publishers and ILS vendors, the EDItEUR/NISO Joint Working Party for the Exchange of Subscription Information (JWP) has proposed a schema for exchanging serials subscription information (Fons et al., 2005). Improved standard identifiers, such as ISBNs and ISSNs, are essential for identifying resources in a digital environment. ISBNs and ISSNs are currently imperfect mechanisms for reliably identifying works in a digital environment. Efforts to enhance these standards may someday improve their reliability as digital identifiers (Jones, 2002).

Resource administration and management

The second primary area of ERM activity is the management of licence and administrative information. Tracking complex licence and administrative information is potentially difficult in the absence of a centralised management system. Licence agreements commonly specify the 'authorised users' who may access a resource, the techniques used to limit access, the responsibilities of the library, remedies for breach, and, in many cases, rights with regard to perpetual access and archival copies. Whether and how materials can be used for electronic reserves, interlibrary loan, or distance education are important licence issues and frequent points of negotiation between libraries and publishers. Administrative information, such as how publisher services can be configured by library staff, who has administrative authority within the local organisation, logins for administrative interfaces, and the location and type of usage data provided by the vendor may also be managed in an ERMS.

Entering licence and administrative information into an ERMS requires informed human intervention to read and interpret agreements and represent licence terms within the ERMS data structure. This is a time-consuming process that requires the expertise of a professional. Rights expression languages (RELs) hold out potential for simplifying this process by providing a machine-to-machine communication of licence and administrative data between contracting partners. The Electronic Resource Management Initiative (ERMI) explored a number of possible REL standards, but concluded that the existing standards will require major modification before they can be applied to library licence agreements. In light of this, the ERMI has proposed that libraries and system vendors develop native XML schema based on the ERMI data set. The effectiveness with which developers implement native XML schemas for rights expression may help to differentiate future ERMS products. XSLT crosswalks of vendor licence data may be needed to facilitate the exchange of licence data.

Managing selection and acquisition

Managing the selection, acquisition and renewal of electronic resources is a complex and time-consuming task. An ERMS can help by providing tools for analysing and comparing the contents of digital resource packages, facilitating cost–usage analysis, tracking the current status of acquisitions and triggering alerts to appropriate staff when action is required, such as a payment or renewal. These tools are useful in any library setting, but are perhaps of greatest value in large organisations where the activities of multiple staff members must be coordinated.

Accurate usage data facilitates the decision-making process of content selectors. The Standardized Usage Statistics Harvesting Initiative (SUSHI) is an effort to develop a standard approach to the machine harvesting of usage data (Jewell and Pesch, 2006). Interest in this new web service is driven largely by the introduction of ERMS software into the library market.

The Electronic Resources Management Initiative

There is at least modest hope that rapid developments in the ERM marketplace will not lead into a labyrinth of idiosyncratic software applications and management strategies. The Digital Library Federation's Electronic Resource Management Initiative (ERMI), launched in 2002, with participation of both librarians and system vendors, has produced 'a series of interrelated documents to define needs and to help establish data standards' for ERM. These documents have been gathered as appendices to the ERMI final report and provide a consistent foundation for ERM development. To one degree or another, most ERMS systems today conform to the ERMI model, although this alone does not guarantee the level of consistency and interoperability that libraries might wish to see.

One of the great strengths of the ERMI report is its comprehensiveness. The key elements of the ERMI include functional requirements for ERM systems, entity-relationship diagrams that map underlying relationships among ERM data, detailed workflows, a data dictionary with over 300 definitions of ERM elements and recommendations for sharing information between ERM systems and data providers. These and other parts of the ERMI have been quickly adopted as guides for ERM development by vendors and libraries.

Whether libraries of every size need an ERMS that meets all of the report's requirements is doubtful. The system envisioned by the ERMI working group is clearly pitched toward the needs of large academic libraries, as are most of the vendor solutions on the market today. Yet for commercial ERMS developers and librarians working on in-house solutions, the ERMI provides an excellent roadmap to development. The ERMI's list of functional requirements and data dictionary are a particularly rich source for system developers. In addition, the proposed XML strategy, if implemented effectively, may offer a migration path from current to future ERM systems.

ERMS types

ERM solutions on the market today are of three fundamental types. Each has the potential to become a comprehensive ERM solution, yet each also has limitations that beg the question of the best path to a successful long-term strategy.

Some ERM solutions function as modules within a closed ILS system. ERM services within a closed ILS have the advantage of compatibility with the native ILS acquisition module. Indeed, the ability to support advanced business transactions may be the distinguishing feature of the ILS model, making it the early front-runner in the ERMS race for many libraries. In situations where technical services staff do the work, the ILS also provides a familiar and consistent user interface.

Relying on a closed ILS may nevertheless have a number of drawbacks. For example, it may compel the library to purchase additional services (illustrated in Figure 6.1) from the ILS vendor. A single vendor thus becomes the library's primary, or even sole, development partner. Looking down the road, this may impose undesirable limitations on service, including the inability to integrate library content easily into a web portal or with other new services outside the ILS. The choice of a closed ILS solution might implicitly rest on the assumption that the ILS bibliographic database will be the catalogue of record for all local information resources, an assumption increasingly under challenge today.

A closed ILS solution can be a relatively quick way to address critical ERM challenges. Typically, however, it also limits choice and results in an overall loss of autonomy, as library services become tightly linked to the software development priorities of the ILS vendor. Because ILS systems are not, as a rule, designed with robust APIs or dynamic exporting capabilities, it is often difficult to integrate ILS solutions with other products or services, as discussed in Chapter 5. These considerations may argue against adopting a closed ILS solution except in cases where business transactions for ERM are of sufficient complexity to require immediate solution. At many libraries, this is reason enough to purchase a closed ILS product.

Standalone or modular ERM solutions

These present another possible avenue for development. When a standalone tool supports well-documented APIs, flexible integration with other ERM services becomes a possibility. A product for managing licence terms and administrative information could thus be integrated with a third-party ILS, link resolver or other service. A third-party web portal might dynamically obtain data from an ERM service through a standard programming interface.

The actual mileage one gets from this approach will vary among implementations, but it is reasonable to foresee advantages. For example, a web services strategy has been adopted by the Ex Libris Verde standalone product. Verde provides a web service API for integration with additional Ex Libris products, such as the SFX link resolver or with other third-party services (Sadeh and Ellingsen, 2005). This opens the door to the type of flexibility that libraries should covet in a period of rapid change, yet there are also possible limitations to consider. A product like Verde can be used in conjunction with the Ex Libris ILS acquisitions module, for example, but integration with the acquisitions module of another ILS will likely be difficult. This decreases the attractiveness of the Verde product for non-Ex Libris customers.

Although other ILS vendors market standalone ERM products, some of these are designed to work only with other modules in the vendor's closed ILS system. The standalone product offered by Innovative Interfaces, for example, lacks open APIs for flexible integration with third-party ERM services. Libraries seeking comprehensive ERM solutions might view this type of standalone product as an initial step toward adopting a new ILS vendor.

Publication access management service solutions

These offer a third model for ERMS development. The core product of a PAMS is journal coverage data that libraries purchase rather than maintain internally. This coverage data provides the springboard from which PAMS providers develop additional ERM services, such as licence management tools and link resolvers.

The PAMS strategy embodies two characteristically Web 2.0 attributes: software as a service and the strategic importance of data (O'Reilly, (2005). Unlike traditional ILS solutions, PAMS like Serials Solutions and TDNet provide a full vessel of content rather than an empty container waiting to be filled. Because coverage data is built into the system, a PAMS can be both cost-effective and easy to implement. At present, these services nevertheless lack the ability to address the acquisitions side of the ERM problem, and offer awkward mechanisms for synchronising data between an ILS or repository and the remotely hosted knowledgebase.

The knowledgebase approach at the heart of the PAMS model is being adopted by other ERM vendor types. The Ex Libris Verde product has always had the 'ability to pre-populate an e-resource database drawing from the SFX central knowledge base' (Davis, 2005). Perhaps in response to numerous complaints about the difficulty of maintaining holdings data, other ERM vendors are following suit and offering the kind of knowledgebase services pioneered by PAMS and link resolver vendors.

Libraries must consider a number of factors when deciding which ERM solutions to pursue, including, most obviously, their existing vendor relationships. For example, a given library may work with a PAMS that offers ERM products that compete with or potentially complement those offered by its ILS vendor. The level of confidence that a library has in existing vendors thus becomes a factor in ERM decisions. In addition to existing vendor relationships, libraries will want to consider:

- The degree to which integration with the library's acquisition module is an ERM priority. Such integration points in the direction of ILS-based services.

- The extent to which flexibility and innovation in front-end discovery tools drives ERM decisions. This typically steers decision makers in the direction of relatively open standalone products or a PAMS solution.

Hybrid approaches to ERM are common. For example, PAMS coverage data is often used to populate an ILS web OPAC or ERM module. This relatively commonplace pairing of an ILS with PAMS data sometimes reveals fault-lines within ERM implementations. An ILS vendor may, for example, use different technology to manage electronic journal coverage data and print journal holdings within the same ERM solution. As of writing, one of the earliest and most successful of ILS solutions uses a MySQL database to track electronic journal coverage data. Print holdings, however, are kept in traditional MARC holdings records. In order to display electronic journal coverage in the OPAC, the library must create traditional serials records that 'virtually' link to records in the e-journal coverage database. Keeping static holdings records coordinated with the more fluid e-journal coverage database is a bothersome task and demonstrates an inelegant linkage between newer more flexible systems and legacy systems.

Willamette case study

Willamette University is among the 20 institutions listed in the ERMI report as a developer of local ERM solutions. The Willamette University experience with ERM development is worth describing here not because it represents a comprehensive ERM solution, but rather because it illustrates some of the inherent tradeoffs in ERM decisions.

Willamette University has from the outset pursued an integrated approach to ERM. Software modules to support such front-end services as a web database gateway, A–Z lists and an OpenURL resolver were written in Perl utilising a MySQL relational database. These services share a common set of administrative back-end tools through which they can be maintained by non-programmers.

Rather than rely on a PAMS, Willamette University has until recently harvested its own coverage data from publishers. In addition, data is automatically loaded on a nightly basis from the ILS into the resolver and A–Z list knowledgebase. Much of the code and the underlying database for these front-end services are shared by a separate ERM module for tracking licence, administrative information, financial information and other aspects of the information lifecycle. This module incorporates most of the relevant fields identified in the ERMI data dictionary.

While working through a series of use cases during the design of the interface for licence and administrative data, it became obvious that the need for a comprehensive ERM licence module was not altogether apparent to Willamette's library staff. In a relatively small library, the kind of extensive functionality recommended by the ERMI exceeds local needs. With a successful front-end service running, further development of modules for licence management and administrative information was placed on hold until demand appeared for these services.

In the intervening two years, a clearer picture of the ERM needs at Willamette University has emerged. A spreadsheet that tracks digitised copies of licence agreements has proven useful. Questions about the use of licensed resources for electronic reserves and interlibrary loan have arisen with some frequency. Librarians have expressed interest the ability to see to basic administrative and access information within the gateway to online databases. They have also expressed an interest in the ability to view title and coverage data by database, a feature that is not currently incorporated into the web portal. Finally, library management is interested in ways to share coverage data and URLs between the resolver knowledgebase and the library's electronic reserves system.

Notably missing from this list of ERM requirements are tools that model the entire lifecycle of an information resource, from selection and acquisition through cancellation. One suspects that these tools would be useful, but within a smaller organisation the time and resources required to implement and manage a solution can ironically undermine productivity. In many cases, informal lines of communication suffice. This may also be true within organisations larger than Willamette University. Yet because ERM is new, we have no authoritative research that shows how libraries of different sizes and types are actually using ERM products today.

Given the success of the Willamette link resolver and A–Z list services, the library eventually decided to begin using a PAMS to obtain most of its coverage data. Modest additions to existing ERM tools are planned for licence and administrative information. At present, no compelling rationale for linking these services to the ILS acquisitions module has been identified and no plans to purchase this functionality are underway. Instead, local ERM efforts will likely focus on closer integration with the electronic reserves service and other public access points.

For the time being, Willamette will continue to support ERM activities through the use of home-grown software. Eventually, a transition to commercial or open source products will occur. Given the recent decision to purchase coverage data from a PAMS, a gradual movement toward these solutions appears to be underway.

Final ERM considerations

The electronic resource management software market is an interesting area of library technology to observe. Managing electronic resources may someday be the primary business of libraries, making ERM systems the ILS of the future. In fact, for a special library that manages electronic journal and book subscriptions exclusively, an ERM system is the only ILS needed today. Because ERM is dependent on large bodies of constantly changing aggregated data, firms that focus on coverage data have gained a foothold in the market and traditional ILS vendors are responding with services that also provide comprehensive coverage data. This trend toward data-centric services has potentially important implications for the future of library services and systems.

Our discussion of ERM emphasises the integration of front-end and back-end services. This point of view is sometimes ignored in other

ERM discussions that, for good and important reasons, focus on immediate management and implementation challenges. Automating existing tasks and achieving efficiencies lie at the core of the ERM problem, and we are still in the early stages of creating effective solutions. Yet ERM also has a strategic role that touches the mission of libraries in fundamental ways. By focusing on the potential of ERM solutions to move a library's digital content into the wider world of networked information – where electronic resources are used and discovered in new ways – we remember the reason why we manage these resources in the first place. Rather than seek the ease of an out-of-the-box solution, it may be smarter to assume that we have a tiger by the tail, and that time, experimentation and flexibility will be required to fix the problem.

Summary

- Electronic resources management is basically different from traditional library practice. These differences arise out of a new legal regime and fundamentally different publishing practices.

- The multiple players in the electronic resources market include subscription agents, publication access management services, content aggregators, publication hosting services, collection publishers and linking services.

- ERM requires integrated solutions for licence management, acquisitions, access control, proxy services, link resolving, web gateways and portals, and federated searching.

- Current ERM systems present a variety of integration strategies, each with strengths and limitations. In choosing a system or systems, libraries must be realistic about both current circumstances and future needs.

- To the greatest extent practical, libraries should be focused on achieving flexible approaches to ERM that maximise the chances of adaptation and innovation.

- Standards related to ERM are under development. As these standards evolve, we are likely to see further changes in ERM systems and services.

7

Digital asset management

Managing the digital assets produced by a library, user community or parent organisation is a new role for librarians that will grow in importance over time. At colleges and universities, the need for digital asset management (DAM) is felt acutely as both instruction and research rely increasingly on digital technology and the knowledge artefacts produced by using this technology. Special libraries facilitate the work of their parent organisations by implementing DAM solutions that contribute to creativity and productivity. Public libraries deliver meaningful civic resources to the community through DAM projects.

Covered in this chapter:

- the challenge of DAM;

- DAM overview;

- the uses of digital assets in academic communities;

- DAM systems by media type;

- strategies for integration.

The digital asset management challenge

Digital asset management is a new and strategically important activity with many practical implications for libraries and their user communities. It is worth noting that DAM is not a technology per se; it is a set of policies and social commitments that define purpose, scope and desired outcomes. Even the question 'what is an asset' must be answered in light of the mission of the institution and the goals that digital assets can help the institution achieve.

DAM addresses fundamentally new information needs that have arisen in the digital environment, and for this reason challenges librarians to think and work creatively. At virtually any library or parent institution there will be multiple opportunities to create and manage digital collections of local materials. Examples include:

- faculty research publications;

- digitised images from historical photograph collections;

- university press or other institutional publications;

- rare books and manuscripts;

- student research and projects;

- historic newspapers;

- video or audio recordings;

- art slide collections;

- scientific datasets;

- learning objects.

These assets have diverse origins. Some are analogue materials that have been digitised for wider dissemination. Others are content created with digital technology and best managed and distributed digitally, such as faculty research publications. Still others are born digital assets, such as multimedia learning objects or websites that have meaning only within a digital environment.

Strategies for managing these assets range from self-archiving to centrally-managed digital collections. E-print repositories of faculty scholarship – sometimes explicitly linked to open-access publishing – are a common example of self-archiving. The self-archiving of reusable teaching and learning objects is of growing interest, especially to faculty and academic departments that use digital content extensively in the classroom. Institutional records management is yet another area of DAM that may potentially include a self-archiving component.

DAM can also be accomplished in a centralised manner. Centrally managed digital repositories require more time and intellectual energy from library and IT organisations. They frequently entail rigorous metadata management, quality control, rights management and preservation policies.

Because centrally managed digital collections represent a larger institutional investment, they are generally reserved for assets that enhance the core mission of the organisation.

There is, however, a porous line between self-archiving and centralised management. In some cases, for example, assets in a centrally managed collection are best understood by content experts or faculty outside the central support organisation. As a consequence, library and IT staff frequently collaborate with content experts who are not trained information professionals. Although this can be a rewarding form of collaboration, the policy structures and support needed for this activity are often ill-defined.

Given these challenges, the development of effective approaches to DAM is a front-burner issue at many institutions. At academic institutions, the need is increasingly driven by faculty and students engaged in the creation of digital content that requires organisation and reuse. As demand for these services continues to grow, DAM may become one of the defining issues for libraries in the twenty-first century.

Crossing boundaries

Clifford Lynch offers one of the more widely quoted definitions of DAM:

> ...[an] institutional repository is a set of services that a university offers to the members of its community for the management and dissemination of digital materials created by the institution and its community members. It is most essentially an organisational commitment to the stewardship of these digital materials, including long-term preservation where appropriate, as well as organisation and access or distribution (Van Westrienen and Lynch, 2005).

Lynch uses the term 'institutional repository' rather than DAM. For the purposes of this chapter, we prefer the broader concept of DAM because it avoids 'collection-centred' assumptions that seem implicit in Lynch's definition. The term 'dissemination', for example, can obscure the full range of services required by a user community. Rather than simply preserve and disseminate assets, DAM initiatives may also respond to complex user needs. This explains why DAM often involves diverse professional viewpoints in its conception and implementation. Librarians, visual resource curators, educational technologists, media professionals, content experts and end-users can each contribute to DAM in related and often interrelated ways.

Because the development of DAM solutions often brings together multiple professional communities, efforts to build common understanding and shared service models may be required. Different professional groups speak different languages and bring unique perspectives to the job. In the short term, professional differences may result in confusion over roles and debates over the paths to follow. Yet with time these differences can lead to more comprehensive and effective approaches to DAM.

Librarians bring an essential perspective to the conversation. As Janz and Giarlo (2005) note, for 'the digital repository, trust involves scholarship, authenticity and persistence over time and has little relationship to immediate financial rewards' or other short term gains. Authenticity and persistence are core values of the library profession and librarians perhaps uniquely understand the practical side of achieving these goals.

DAM thus requires knowledge and leadership from library professionals. For librarians, DAM in turn requires an exploration of roles and forms of collaboration that may be new and unfamiliar.

DAM overview

Before going further, we should discuss the broader framework within which local DAM activities occur. Figure 7.1, adapted from a diagram developed by OCLC staff, offers an overview of DAM within academic and research communities (Dempsey et al., 2005). At the centre of the diagram are the institutional repositories to which Lynch refers in the definition above. The existence of multiple repositories is important to note. Rather than a single database that meets the needs of a user community, multiple repositories are the generally-accepted framework for DAM, due in part to the range of media types and uses discussed later in this chapter.

The diagram's two-dimensional layout seems to imply a clustered group of repositories hosted by a single institution, ringed by a well-defined user community on the one hand and third-party data services on the other. This would roughly mimic the role of the traditional library catalogue in university settings. In reality, however, DAM is far more three-dimensional. The repositories shown in the diagram may

Figure 7.1 Digital asset management overview

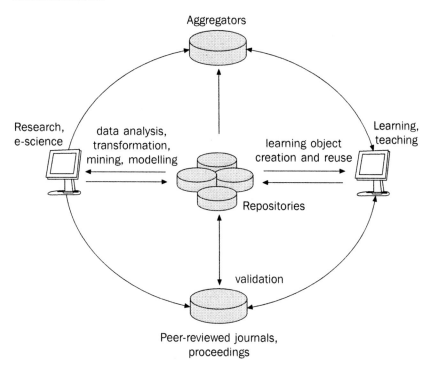

Aggregators

Research, e-science

data analysis, transformation, mining, modelling

learning object creation and reuse

Learning, teaching

Repositories

validation

Peer-reviewed journals, proceedings

exist within local, consortial, national or international settings (Peters, 2002). The emerging model of DAM thus envisions local data repositories that participate in a broader network of scholarly and educational activity.

The areas of user activity represented in Figure 7.1 are research and e-science on the one hand, and learning and teaching on the other. Each of these activities relies to varying degrees on local or non-local data sources. A researcher, for example, might obtain geographic information system (GIS) data from national repositories, but store locally enhanced datasets within a campus institutional repository. Data stored in the local repository will in turn be available to researchers at the host institution and to a global disciplinary community. Interoperability between repository services and metadata facilitate this global framework for research and teaching.

The discovery of materials within this distributed environment is supported by meta-repositories that aggregate content, and by federated search protocols that enable searches across multiple repositories. The aggregators shown in Figure 7.1 harvest metadata from other repositories, typically using the Open Archives Initiative Protocol for Metadata Harvesting (OAI-PMH) described in Chapter 3. These OAI aggregation services may be offered by research libraries, library consortia, disciplinary associations, non-profit societies and other governmental and non-governmental agencies. The OAIster project of the University of Michigan Digital Library Production Service is a leading example of an aggregation service. Search engines like Google are also exploring the use of OAI to harvest repository metadata. Federated searches across multiple repositories may use SRU/W or the OpenSearch protocol. Each of these protocols is described in Chapter 3.

The final component of DAM in Figure 7.1 illustrates the role that institutional repositories may play in the scholarly communication process. The Open Access Initiative and related efforts to reform scholarly communication advocate the use of institutional repositories for self-archiving of refereed journal articles.[1] To date, however, institutional repositories of faculty publications have inspired limited faculty participation, with self-archiving generally more successful when required for faculty assessment or by grant-funding agencies (van Westrienen and Lynch, 2005). Libraries are recognising the limits of an appeal to enlightened self-interest and are taking additional steps to encourage self-archiving within the academic community (Foster and Gibbons, 2005).

Taken together, the services illustrated in Figure 7.1 constitute an emerging communications framework in which local DAM activities play an integral part. This framework is global, and includes such notably large players as Google and Yahoo, each of which currently functions as an aggregator of repository content. Niche players serve as repositories and aggregators for specific user communities.

As potential players in this emerging framework, libraries face distinct challenges. Local digital collections can be built without reference to other collections at the regional, national and international levels, but strong incentives exist for broader integration of resources into a global networked environment. In the digital world, small and independent collections are simply less valuable than large aggregations, a lesson that is daily demonstrated by Google and Yahoo. Incompatible silos of data effectively hide digital assets from all but the most lucky or persistent of information seekers.

The malleable nature of digital content presents yet another challenge. Meaningful access to a digital resource often entails more than discovering, viewing and printing. Consider an instructor who locates digital images within a library-supported repository, then incorporates these images into a classroom presentation that is itself a new multimedia learning object. As this example shows, the creation of new digital artefacts is more than just a secondary or derivative outcome; it is one of the primary rationales for DAM. From the digital library point of view, this typically means that DAM strategies must play well with other software applications.

Collection-centered DAM

At most parent institutions, librarians are among the natural leaders of DAM initiatives. They understand collection management, preservation, metadata and taxonomies and have technical expertise in managing and converting data. They also hold the keys to special collections, archives, dissertations and other materials that are prime candidates for digitisation and fertile ground for testing and developing DAM solutions.

Librarians tend to instinctively approach DAM through the lens of time-honoured traditions and practices that are collection-centred by nature. Collection-centred DAM is complex and challenging, but also familiar in its general outlines. Its primary foci are preservation and access.

Preservation of digital materials for future reuse is a significant, long-term commitment to the user community. It requires plans for backups and disaster recovery, maintenance and storage of archival file formats, refreshing files on a periodic basis and migration to new data formats as needed. Clearly understood preservation policies are essential for preservation, as reflected in the almost monumental *Data Dictionary for Preservation Metadata: Final Report of the PREMIS Working Group* (OCLC, 2005), developed under the sponsorship of OCLC and the Research Library Group (RLG).

Access to content is facilitated by digitisation, descriptive metadata and search interfaces. In the case of rare books and manuscripts, for example, libraries provide digital surrogates that expand the potential audience for these materials and bring greater visibility to the parent institution. E-print archives like the Cornell University sponsored arXiv collection of papers in physics, mathematics, computer science and quantitative biology offer clearinghouses for communication within academic disciplines. In these and similar cases, the role of a repository service ends at the close of an HTTP GET request.

Beyond the collection

This collection-centred approach to DAM achieves necessary and important outcomes. But it fails to meet all the needs of local repository users. The limits of a purely collection-centred approach to DAM are illustrated by the predicament of art historians and visual resource librarians as they negotiate the transition from analogue to digital images.

Access to art images is essential for teaching art history and, until recently, a well-catalogued collection of analogue slides, teamed up with carousel slide projectors, had served the needs of art history instruction for decades. The recent shift to digital images upsets the art history applecart in several ways. In addition to a well-organised and searchable collection of digital images, art history instruction with digital images also requires:

- integrating digital images into classroom lectures that utilise software presentation tools;

- incorporating images from multiple repositories into a single lecture and thus into the same piece of presentation software;

- access tools designed to aid in assessing image quality as well as content;

- software upgrades as well as training and support in the use of software, hardware and projectors in the classroom;

- student access to the images presented in class and effective study tools.

Any DAM strategy that addresses these needs must consider both collection management issues and the intended use of data. This close integration between content, presentation and learning activities expands the focus of a DAM initiative.

Or consider a small set of digitised letters from a university archive that were written during the American Civil War. Such collections are scattered across the USA at colleges, universities and historical societies. Many of these collections are insubstantial on their own and of possibly limited local interest. But through a technology like OAI metadata harvesting, digitised versions of these letters can be incorporated into a more extensive scholarly repository of Civil War materials. Within the context of this aggregated scholarly portal, once insignificant and hidden letters take on added importance, the scholarly equivalent of the 'long tail' phenomenon, in which the value of many seldom-used items outweighs that of a few popular bestsellers (Anceson, 2004).

A Civil War letter project might be undertaken entirely by library staff as a kind of collection-centred initiative. Yet it is also an opportunity to enlist the help of historians and history students who can investigate the context in which the letters were written, or the precise locations and events described therein. Students or faculty might also contribute to transcriptions that enable full-text searching. Such collaboration is itself a form of scholarship and pedagogy not unlike the Valley of the Shadow Project, in which historians developed web-based resources and subsequently enlisted the help of the libraries at the University of Virginia.

In each of these examples, opportunities to combine content from multiple collections (interoperability) and incorporate this content into teaching and study tools (malleability) are not the logical outcome of traditional collection-centred thinking. They emerge instead from the needs of users and new forms of collaboration that draw library practice out into a blended environment characterised by user-centred approaches to planning and innovation.

DAM system basics

Given the multifaceted nature of DAM, it is hardly surprising to find a wide range of DAM software solutions. Many of these solutions address the needs of specific user communities, as outlined above. Others trace their origin to the media that they were designed to manage, as described in the following section. Yet all comprehensive DAM systems share certain characteristics.

The best roadmap to a comprehensive DAM solution is provided by the Open Archival Information System (OAIS) reference model. As a reference model, OAIS provides 'common terms and concepts for describing repository architectures and comparing implementations' of DAM solutions (RLG, 2003).[2] The functions supported by OAIS compliant systems are the ability to:

- *Ingest* materials submitted by a content provider, extract file information associated with the digital object and prepare the digital object for further cataloguing and archival activities. A simple example of this would be importing a series of photographic images into the DAM archive, extracting relevant file information included in the digital file headers (such as file type, date created and file size) and presenting the images and associated data to the collection maintainer for further descriptive cataloguing.

- *Archive* materials, including facilities to assure complete backup, disaster recovery and migration of archival materials to new storage media and file formats in the future.

- *Manage* data, including controlled vocabularies or schemas. The system must respond to search queries by users and ideally allow the collection manager to define which metadata fields are indexed and searchable. In a production environment like a library or archive, the system must also generate reports on metadata within the archive and permit collection-level or selective updates.

- *Administer* repository functions, including an ability to define authorisation levels for content producers, manage processing workflow, monitor system status and facilitate rights management or support e-commerce.

- *Preserve* content through file refreshing and migration to new formats. DAM systems for long-term archiving should facilitate the use of administrative metadata to record information about the creation and provenance of digital objects, as well as tools that help to track objects and apply preservation policies.

- *Access* to digital resources and effective presentation to the user. This may include conversion of archival files, such as TIFF, to a presentation format, such as JPEG. When structural metadata is used to define compound object files (such as a monograph composed of multiple page images) the system may need to translate these compound object files into navigable web documents that can be viewed in a web browser.

DAM solutions for different media

Within most settings, a variety of digital media need to be managed. At the time of writing, however, most software solutions for DAM are designed either primarily or exclusively with one type of media in mind. There are significant exceptions to this rule, but more often than not these exceptions betray a subtle media bias. Developing an effective

DAM strategy therefore involves choices about when to adopt distinct or complementary software solutions for different media and when to rely instead on crossover solutions.

Digital text

The open access movement has spawned some of the most interesting and successful examples of repository services oriented toward textual information. The eScholarship repository of the University of California system, for example, uses the Digital Commons repository system developed by bePress and marketed and hosted by ProQuest. The bePress suite of products includes services for dissertations, peer-reviewed scholarly journal publications, or conference proceedings. The Digital Commons repository shares the same underlying architecture as these other bePress services, each of which is designed specifically for print publications. Among the useful text-oriented features of the Digital Commons repository is the ability to translate word-processed documents into PDF for repository storage, as well as full-text searching of repository contents.

The primary open source competitors for commercial repository services like bePress are DSpace, developed jointly by the Massachusetts Institute of Technology and Hewlett Packard, and EPrints, developed at the University of Southampton. Neither DSpace nor EPrints currently support the type of full-text searching offered by Digital Commons. EPrints is strongly oriented toward open-access publishing and as such is a good fit for DAM initiatives that focus on research publications. EPrints can be configured to support other media types, but most existing implementations contain only textual materials. Images, data sets and other media types are more common in DSpace repositories, yet the DSpace package reflects much of the same bias toward research publications that is evident in EPrints and Digital Commons.

Despite obvious strengths, these repository services share certain basic limitations. Among these are an absence of facilities for browsing still images or video, and specialised tools for ingesting and indexing visual media.

Digital images

Other applications currently on the market are designed primarily or exclusively to manage digital images. Some of these image management systems were created with a very specific audience in mind. The open source MDID2 image management software, created at James Madison University, and the commercially available Luna Insight, are applications designed expressly for the needs of art history instruction. Other image management solutions were designed with photographers and media professionals in mind and are particularly helpful when managing large quantities of images produced through digital photography.

The Mellon-funded ARTStor project is a significant repository of art images that may also factor into local decisions about image management. ARTStor is, in the first instance, an image database that provides rich and extensive image collections and software for teaching with these images in the classroom. More recently, ARTStor has introduced a hosting service for image collections that are owned or controlled by local institutions (the subject matter of these images is not limited to art). ARTStor thus becomes a factor in DAM planning for any institution that subscribes to the product.

CONTENTdm, developed originally at the University of Washington and now a commercial product, is primarily used to manage image collections but also supports a variety of archival collections, including rare books and manuscripts. Like DSpace, CONTENTdm may be used successfully with a variety of media, but its strengths as an asset management and presentation tool make it a prime candidate for image archive initiatives. CONTENTdm does not provide the advanced presentation tools offered by ARTStor, Luna or MDID2, but compensates with superior tools for collection management, workflow, preservation of master copies, and discovery across multiple collections. Unlike DSpace, CONTENTdm supports a centralised approach to content creation, and thus lends itself more naturally to library and archival operations.

Video and audio

Audio and, to a much larger degree, video present unique challenges for DAM, including greater storage requirements than other media and an absence of standardised file formats. Nevertheless, significant DAM applications are being developed for these media. One example is the open source Video Tools project at the Harvard Business School, the goal of which is to provide 'capture, storage and delivery mechanisms' in addition to 'an instructor-accessible means to access, search and repurpose video assets based on content as well as easy-to-use tools for creating mixed-media presentations'.[3] The Harvard open source project includes tools for automatically capturing metadata from video, which can then be used to extract relevant clips from longer video segments. Advanced features, such as automated metadata extraction, are computationally difficult relative to other media types. At this point in time, video repositories are the subject of intensive research and development, much of it funded by the National Science Foundation (NSF), including the NSF-funded Carnegie Mellon University Informedia Project.

Crossover examples: DSpace and CONTENTdm

Almost any repository solution can be used to deliver multiple media types, if only because the services over which repositories operate – file servers and web servers, for example – are capable of delivering any type of data. Yet for a solution to accommodate multiple media types effectively, the generic ability to deliver bit-streams must be augmented by metadata and indexing capabilities, management tools and search interfaces appropriate for multiple media types.

Some repository services do have crossover potential. We noted above that many DSpace implementations contain images, data sets and other media types. Although DSpace development initially emphasised research publications as the representative content type within a DSpace repository, the system is designed around user communities rather than a particular mode of publication. This community-oriented model tends to moderate any inherited media bias.

In contrast to the DSpace community-oriented model, CONTENTdm is a centralised management solution clearly designed with still images in mind. Many of its most notable interface features facilitate image presentation and browsing. As with DSpace and other more generalised repository solutions, however, CONTENTdm developers make efforts to accommodate other media types. The addition of OCR capabilities for full-text indexing is an indication of this philosophy. The ability to link images into compound objects that mimic the structure of a monograph and permit browsing individual page images as parts of a book or newspaper makes CONTENTdm appropriate for many textual publications. CONTENTdm may be ideal for creating digital newspapers and rare books collections that can be browsed visually and searched textually for intellectual content.

Given their multimedia features, CONTENTdm and DSpace are two examples of crossover repository solutions that can be used quite effectively for more than one media type.

Comprehensive models: Fedora

Because different media have different characteristics and uses, multiple repository implementations probably make sense for most institutions. At the same time, repositories have many traits in common, as is illustrated in the OAIS model. An underlying repository framework that supports a wide range of media types and uses might therefore be beneficial in the long term.

The Fedora open source software project, developed jointly by Cornell University Information Science and the University of Virginia Library, provides one possible path to this future. Fedora is a highly generalised repository architecture. The strength of the Fedora framework resides in a single, robust repository upon which various specialised digital collection services can be built. Such services include cataloguing and workflow tools, interfaces for accessing and browsing repository contents, package submission tools, etc. The Fedora open source framework is available to both commercial software vendors and in-house developers working at a single institution or in a collaborative arrangement across institutions. Among the numerous applications of Fedora are the following (Fedora Development Team, 2005):

- The ARROW Project (Australia) and DEFF Project are using Fedora to build institutional repositories for the storage and dissemination of scholarly literature.

- The integrated library system vendor VTLS has built a repository solution suitable for a variety of media and has also contributed an electronic theses and dissertations submission tool (called Valet) back to the open source Fedora community.

- Yale University and Tufts University are creating a Fedora-based system for the storage and preservation of electronic university records.

- Tufts University is developing a repository for educational technologies with enhanced interoperability through application programming interfaces developed at MIT as part of the Open Knowledge Initiative for learning object repositories.

- The Electronic Encyclopedia of Chicago, developed by the Chicago Historical Society and Northwestern University, uses Fedora to deliver a hyperlinked resource of maps, images and text.

- A number of university research libraries including the University of Virginia, Tufts University, the National Library of Wales and the University of Athens (Greece) are using Fedora to host and deliver digital collections.

- The National Science Digital Library is a National Science Foundation project that is using Fedora to store an information network overlay that represents content, metadata, agents, services and annotations for its multi-portal digital library.

- Under the sponsorship of National Institute for Technology and Liberal Education, computer science students have developed ELATED, an easy to use front end for Fedora which makes the functionality of Fedora available to small colleges.

These examples show the extensive range of applications that can be created using the Fedora repository.

Perhaps the key feature of Fedora is its flexible object model. According to Lagoze et al. (2005), 'the Fedora object model supports the expression of many kinds of complex objects, including documents, images, electronic books, multi-media learning objects, datasets, computer programs and other compound information entities'. Media types can be aggregated in any combination to form complex objects, and objects can be associated with services or programs with the ability to produce content dynamically. Fedora also supports many of the metadata standards discussed later in this chapter.

Another key strength of Fedora is that it runs as a web service; all repository services can be accessed through REST and SOAP interfaces. This means that Fedora can be integrated into multiple application environments with distinctly different user interfaces (Fedora Development Team, 2005).

The Fedora model demonstrates that a single digital repository framework can be applied to a variety of distinct needs and goals through a multi-tiered application approach. In the long term, this model could simultaneously enhance the interoperability of digital archives and reduce the need for multiple standalone DAM systems. Further vendor support for Fedora or Fedora-like solutions seems likely in the future. Meanwhile, as a DAM strategy, Fedora will continue to require considerably more programming support than will out-of-the box solutions.

Metadata

When librarians think of metadata what comes most naturally to mind is *descriptive metadata*, such as title, author or subject. Effective use of descriptive metadata will indeed be one of the hallmarks of successful DAM. Yet in addition to descriptive metadata, two additional types of metadata play essential roles. *Administrative metadata* facilitates rights management, preservation and documentation of software requirements. Without administrative metadata, the maintenance of long-term digital archives would be impossible. In addition, digital assets frequently require *structural metadata* that expresses relationships between individual digital files. Structural metadata can be used, for example, to create complex digital objects that combine multiple digital files and associated metadata. Obvious uses of structural metadata include binding together separate page images into a virtual monograph or pairing a page image and its textual transcription.

A number of metadata standards are particularly important for repository development:

- XML provides the universal syntax used by DAM systems. A more complete overview of XML is provided in Chapter 3. XML is a subset of the SGML markup language that is used extensively by web applications to encode, manage and transmit data.

- MARCXML, developed and maintained by the Library of Congress, provides a framework for expressing full MARC records in XML. Because the protocol is capable of rendering completely the highly structured MARC record format, there are many possible uses of MARCXML in a library environment. Most DAM systems do not support MARCXML natively, but style sheets can be used to transform MARCXML into other native metadata formats like Dublin Core, Qualified Dublin Core and MODS.

- MODS (Metadata Object Description Schema) is a simplified version of the MARC standard expressed in XML. Because MODS is derived from MARC and provides a container for hierarchical, structured metadata, in contrast to the flat Dublin Core framework, it is more compatible with library applications. A number of repository software applications are developing MODS support.

- The Dublin Core metadata set is comprised of 15 elements that can be applied to a broad range of resources and shared across many disciplines and organisations. Although unqualified Dublin Core elements lack the specificity and precision of other metadata schemes, they nevertheless provide a general framework onto which other, more precise metadata elements can be mapped. By providing a common denominator, Dublin Core facilitates the meaningful sharing of metadata between repositories, thus increasing metadata interoperability and opening the door to resource discovery across diverse domains. Dublin Core is the most frequently used descriptive metadata standard supported by DAM systems and is a requirement of resource sharing via the OAI metadata harvesting protocol. In addition to the 15 basic data elements of Simple Dublin Core, Qualified Dublin Core introduces qualifiers that can significantly increase the specificity of metadata expressed in Dublin Core. Qualified Dublin Core is the native metadata scheme of DSpace and CONTENTdm, among other systems.

- EAD (Encoded Archival Description) is designed for encoding archival finding aids, inventories and other record types created by archives, museums and libraries. EAD provides collection-level description of archival materials. Some DAM systems, including CONTENTdm, have the ability to ingest and display EAD records.

- METS (Metadata Encoding and Transmission Standard) provides an XML standard for wrapping descriptive, structural and administrative metadata together within a single record. Each of the XML-based standards mentioned above (Dublin Core, MarcXML, MODS and EAD) can be incorporated into a METS record as descriptive metadata. DAM systems that utilise METS include DSpace and Fedora.

Given the significant challenge of preserving digital materials, successful long-term DAM initiatives also require standards for file formats. Common examples of this include TIFF or JPEG2000 for images and WAV or MPEG for audio files. Typically non-proprietary, standard file formats accomplish two things: they maximise the useful life of digital content and greatly simplify migration to new file formats and new generations of computer technology.

Integration with digital libraries

The integration of digital repositories with each other and with other library services is a significant challenge. Consider a repository that contains faculty publications. If these titles are of sufficient interest to a local user community, there may be reason to add them to the library catalogue. Manual cataloguing of these titles would be one option. A possibly more efficient approach is to harvest Dublin Core metadata from the repository and translate the data into MARC records. This MARC record data could then be added to the library catalogue.

Metadata translation is in fact quite common in today's networked information environment. Unlike the traditional world of bibliographic services for print, where MARC is the common language for cataloguers and integrated library systems alike, multiple languages are necessary in the world of networked information.

Translation between metadata standards is therefore essential, and typically referred to as a metadata crosswalk. There are as many crosswalks as there are one-to-one permutations of descriptive metadata standards.

We have already described commonly used metadata standards, ranging from MARCXML, a standard that faithfully encodes of every detail in a MARC record, to Dublin Core, a vastly simplified standard with a limited capacity to express complex bibliographic information. Translation from a complex to a simple metadata schema is often referred to as a 'lossy' translation because many distinctions in the complex record are lost when mapped onto a smaller set of metadata fields.

In the example above, translation of simple Dublin Core into highly structured MARC will therefore yield correspondingly simple MARC records. Ambiguities present in relatively unstructured Dublin Core metadata might be addressed during the translation process through custom programming – assuming these ambiguities can be addressed at all.

The simplicity of Dublin Core is nevertheless its greatest strength, because it facilitates information discovery across a diverse universe of repositories. Incompatible descriptive information about author, composer, artist, or researcher from multiple repositories can be mapped to the Dublin Core 'creator' field and shared with other repositories via this least common denominator. This virtue has made Dublin Core mandatory in the OAI metadata harvesting protocol. Yet the simplicity of Dublin Core is also a significant weakness, as many metadata needs cannot be addressed in native Dublin Core alone.

If a repository service supports the MODS metadata standard, a richer translation of data is possible. MODS data can be included in Dublin Core records exported by an OAI service. In the example above, a repository of faculty publications might thus export Dublin Core that has been enhanced with MODS descriptors. A translation from MODS to MARC would then produce correspondingly richer records for the library catalogue. Repository developers like DSpace are currently developing the ability to deliver MODS data via METS and OAI export.

Crosswalks between metadata formats can be accomplished in a variety of ways. Perhaps the most common technique uses XSLT translation. XSLT translation requires an XSLT style sheet and XSLT translation software. When an appropriate style sheet is applied to an incoming stream of XML encoded metadata, the XSLT translator will produce a new XML document in the target metadata format.

Data interoperability between repositories is a complex challenge that will occupy the attention of the digital library community for some time to come. Yet at the local level, digital library integrators also face distinctly user-driven needs for interoperability. Consider this example: a library purchases a set of art slides and incorporates these slides into a repository service, such as CONTENTdm. The art history faculty, however, use the open source MDID2 application in the classroom. These individuals need a convenient way to export data from CONTENTdm into MDID2. How might this happen?

One possible answer is to use the technologies described here and elsewhere in this book to automate the transfer of metadata from CONTENTdm to MDID2. A PHP generated link in CONTENTdm might pass item data to a locally developed web service. This service could use the CONTENTdm OAI interface to request the item metadata and images. Metadata could then be translated into a format suitable for MDID2 and sent to that application. Image translation may also be required. Once within the MDID2 repository, faculty can conveniently incorporate images into classroom lectures.

The strategic role of DAM

DAM is an integral part of broader developments in education, research and scholarly communication that will shape libraries for the foreseeable future. Over time, some of these broader developments may diminish traditional library roles. For example, nothing in recent memory has created more shelf-capacity in academic libraries than the removal of journal titles available through subscription to services like JSTOR. Journals accessed through the digital archives of publishers are amenable to centralised management and preservation strategies. The question of who maintains the journal archive in a digital era therefore looms large. Whether it will be publishers, library consortia, non-profit associations or for-profit digitisation and indexing initiatives by companies like Google or Yahoo is unclear. Yet whatever the solution, the shift from ownership to access is outsourcing roles that have traditionally been the province of local libraries (Waters, 2005).

Meanwhile, the DAM problem first articulated in the corporate setting is continuing to proliferate within the communities that libraries serve. The mission of libraries to preserve and provide access to information might therefore accommodate a strategic turn toward DAM. Academic libraries, for example, may anticipate a growing demand by faculty and students for better access to such local digital materials as faculty image collections, multimedia learning objects, theses and other student works. Faculty may welcome or demand collaboration on new types of digital scholarly endeavour. Archives and special collection units may demonstrate the ability of digitisation initiatives to create a wider audience for the visual and historical resources within their collections. Public libraries and museums may unlock this same potential. Each of these activities furthers the core mission of the library. In many cases they also provide significant public relations benefits to the parent institution.

Libraries that undertake digital collection initiatives must weigh costs and benefits and to some extent review their audience and mission. The implications for staffing are significant. In many settings, DAM will require new relationships with educational technologists and other technology support staff within the parent organisation. Digital collections will almost certainly entail a close and ongoing collaboration between systems staff, cataloguers, archivists, museum curators, visual resource librarians, media librarians, faculty and other content creators. Ultimately, unless new staff can be added, DAM will take time and energy away from other activities. As sometimes happens when professional roles are caught up in change, there may be bouts with what Thorstein Veblen (1914) called 'trained incapacity', in which past ways of working and thinking hinder our ability to develop new strategies adapted to present need. These administrative and cultural issues have significant implications for DAM. Yet for the foreseeable future, DAM is likely to be a growing and unavoidable concern for the communities that libraries serve.

Summary

- Demand for DAM solutions is being driven by the impact of technology on research and learning. This demand is driven by the need to organise and reuse locally produced digital content.

- Libraries are natural leaders in developing DAM solutions. This is because of their professional expertise as collection managers and their strategic position as the keepers of many of their institution's intellectual assets.

- A collection-centred approach to DAM will not meet all demands. A user-centred approach that involves librarians in new roles is essential.

- Collaboration between librarians, educational technologists, faculty and others is essential for successful DAM.

- The selection of DAM software solutions will reflect numerous considerations, including the nature of various digital media and the use to which digital assets will be put.

- Local DAM activities are an integral part of an emerging international framework for scholarly communication and education.

- The integration of local repositories with regional, national and international repositories will be a defining measure of success. Metadata standards and metadata translations are essential to meeting this goal.

Notes

1. For an overview of the open access concept see the 'Budapest Open Access Initiative', available at: *http://www.soros.org/openaccess/ read.shtml* (accessed: 25 January 2006).
2. For a more in depth discussion of OAIS, see Committee for Space Data Systems (2002).
3. See: *http://www.provost.harvard.edu/it_fund moreinfo_grants.php? id=31* (accessed: 18 February 2006).

8

Integration with content providers

Until the final years of the twentieth century, libraries satisfied the vast majority of patron information needs with locally owned books, journals and other resources. The rise of the Internet changed that model of library services forever. By making it convenient for users to access information produced and maintained thousands of miles away, the Internet shifted the focus of libraries from ownership to access. While still maintaining a print collection, most libraries are purchasing more and more electronic resources to satisfy patron needs. It is now common for libraries to subscribe to dozens or even hundreds of externally hosted databases containing articles, books, maps, images, video and other resources.

Covered in this chapter:

- technologies useful for identifying and obtaining known items;

- technologies that facilitate information discovery;

- the influence of search engines on digital libraries;

- methods to develop local integration solutions.

Electronic collections typically consist of a dynamically changing array of resources that is maintained by disparate vendors, libraries and consortia. When libraries first started delivering services over the Web, the initial solution for integrating content was simply to provide a web page with links to the various resources. For small electronic collections, this method works reasonably well. But a set of simple hyperlinks to separate silos of data does not address two fundamental integration needs: (1) the ability to find out if a digital library can provide a known resource, such as a journal article, and (2) the ability to perform a search for a topic of interest across several separate information sources at once.

Content integration technologies thus fall into two broad categories. The first category consists of protocols that make it possible to retrieve known items, such as specific journal articles or book titles. These technologies are useful when a library patron knows of a resource because they have a reference from a bibliography in a book, a citation in an article or because they have found a citation in the results of a search in an online database. OpenURL and digital object identifiers (DOIs) both fall into this category because they allow users to gain access or 'deep link' to a particular resource that they know they want. Generally speaking, tools in this category are relatively simple and inexpensive to implement.

The second category contains integration technologies devoted to information discovery. These allow users to concurrently search multiple subscription and non-subscription databases for unknown items, such as articles, books on a particular topic or all works by a particular author. Examples of such technologies include federated searching standards, such as Z39.50 and SRU/W. Internet search engines index data on other systems, so they effectively allow users to search multiple systems even though few of them offer true federated search capabilities. Sophistication and cost of information discovery tools vary widely.

OpenURL

OpenURL deserves special mention because it is the first widely supported protocol that links abstracting and full-text databases, electronic journals, interlibrary loan systems, online public access catalogues (OPACs) and other resources. Library patrons frequently use OpenURL without being aware of it. When patrons use web-based databases like PsychArticles, Historical Abstracts, Web of Science or Anthropological Index, they often are presented with the option of clicking on a link labelled something like 'Get Item', 'Get at My Library', 'SFX', etc. This link is a specially formatted URL that contains information about the item. Clicking on the link typically passes this information to a link resolver that gives the patron options for acquiring the book or article in question.

As its name implies, OpenURL uses a uniform resource locator (URL) to transfer bibliographic information over the Web. A URL is simply a web address. Although a URL can be used to retrieve information from a web address, it can also be used to send information *to* a web address. This means that URLs can be used to execute queries in databases, generate maps with driving directions and perform a wide variety of other common tasks. Most users of the Web are familiar with long URLs that contain lots of data. OpenURL is a standard for encoding bibliographic data within such URLs. By making it possible to transmit bibliographic information with a simple web address, OpenURL makes it possible to move citation data from one web application to another.[1]

OpenURLs were originally conceived in the late 1990s by Herbert Von De Sompel and his colleagues at the University of Ghent in Belgium (van de Sompel, 2001). Library content providers and automation vendors readily adopted the 0.1 version of the OpenURL standard in the early 2000s. National Information Standards Organisation (NISO)'s Committee AX revised the initial OpenURL specification so that it could be applied to objects other than scholarly citations (Hendricks, 2003). Version 1.0 of the OpenURL standard was approved by NISO and ANSI in April 2005 as NISO/ANSI Z39.88 2004 (NISO, 2005).

The OpenURL specification published by NISO is difficult reading for anyone who is not an information specialist with systems experience, but OpenURL is a simple protocol to understand and implement. For the purposes of understanding the OpenURL concept, let us examine a simple 0.1 version OpenURL:

http://resolver.university.edu?sid=ABCCLIO:HA&genre=article& aulast=Payne&epage=314&spage=312&issue=3&volume=34& date=1962&issn=00222801&title=Journal%20of%20Modern %20History&atitle=RECENT%20STUDIES%20ON%20THE% 20SPANISH%20CIVIL%20WAR.

By breaking the OpenURL down into its parts and removing the URL encoding (the ampersands which separate name/value pairs and '%20s', which simply represent spaces), we can better understand how it works.

http://resolver.university.edu
sid=ABCCLIO:HA
genre=article
aulast=Payne

```
epage=314
spage=312
date=1962
issn=00222801
title=Journal of Modern History
atitle=RECENT STUDIES ON THE SPANISH CIVIL WAR
```

The service component, resolver or 'base URL' of the OpenURL (*http:// resolver.university.edu*) points to the server that processes the URL. The remainder of the OpenURL contains metadata about the resource. In the example above we can easily identify the metadata elements that are present: the ISSN number follows 'issn=', the article title follows 'atitle=', and so on.

Version 1.0 of the OpenURL extends these capabilities so that the OpenURL can be used for objects other than intellectual works. It also provides more defined areas for metadata about the object in question and the services desired. It breaks down the metadata in the OpenURL into several subsections including the:

- *referent*: the object being referenced; typically, this is the journal article, book, etc that one seeks to acquire;

- *referring entity*: the database entry, article, book, etc. referring to the object one seeks to acquire;

- *referrer*: the service providing the referral;

- *requester*: the person requesting the object;

- *resolver*: the program that interprets the OpenURL;

- *service type*: the type of service requested by the user of the OpenURL; for example, the full text on an article.

It also provides for a 'registry' area of the OpenURL to identify the version of the OpenURL standard, the character encoding used, the metadata format used (appropriate to the genre: book, journal, dissertation, etc.) and other information (NISO, 2005). As of this writing, adoption of the 1.0 OpenURL standard is proving to be slow, with some vendors utilising hybrid OpenURLs that attempt to follow the syntax of both standards. As OpenURL lets different vendors and organisations know how information will arrive, they can easily develop tools that allow systems to work together.

OpenURL resolvers

One of the most obvious applications for OpenURL in a library setting is to connect citations for articles with the full text of that article. In order to accomplish this, an OpenURL resolver is used. An OpenURL resolver is simply a program that offers options for acquiring an article, book or other item via an electronic source, a reference in a library catalogue or an interlibrary loan request.

The most common use for an OpenURL resolver is to point users to articles in electronic journals. To link users to electronic journal articles, an OpenURL resolver must:

- Contain a database (or 'knowledgebase') of library holdings. Typically, this database contains a row for every instance of an electronic journal from a particular provider. The row typically holds the following data: journal title, journal publisher/aggregator (e.g. EbscoHost, ScienceDirect), ISSN number, years of coverage, and URL to a web page from which the journal may be browsed/searched.

- Know the 'target' linking syntax to deep link to articles at various electronic journal providers' websites. Some vendors support the OpenURL syntax, others use the DOI and still others use their own idiosyncratic format. Some vendors don't allow direct linking to a particular article and thus the resolver can only return a 'title level' link to an electronic journal.

- Be able to extract information from outside sources as appropriate to generate links. For example, a resolver may need to consult the CrossRef service to acquire the DOI for a particular article if a DOI is required to make a target link.

OpenURL resolvers are typically used as follows: on finding an article of interest in a research database, the information seeker obtains the article by clicking on the OpenURL attached to it. Upon clicking on the OpenURL, the user is directed from the database vendor's web server to a server controlled by the local library. This is the OpenURL resolver or link server.

At this point, the resolver checks the metadata sent via OpenURL (author, journal title, date, etc.) against its knowledgebase to see if the library can provide access to the article. If the resolver's knowledgebase indicates that the library provides electronic access to the resource, it constructs links to the full text of the article and/or links to holdings for the printed version of a journal. If the library does not have access to the article desired, the resolver might offer to transfer the metadata on to an interlibrary loan request system.

Libraries seeking to take advantage of OpenURL technology must first acquire a resolver unless they wish to funnel all requests through an OpenURL compliant interlibrary loan system. There are many choices available for resolver products and the market is competitive. Ferguson (2004) compared 11 different resolver products. Six of the products were offered by traditional automation vendors while the remaining five were offered by publication access management services (Serials Solutions and TDNet), a specialised library technology company (Openly Informatics), and two research database vendors (Ebsco and Ovid). The entry of so many firms into the market, especially non-integrated library system vendors, has pushed prices down. Libraries looking to purchase a resolver should be selective and take advantage of their strong bargaining position.

When looking for a resolver, libraries should consider several factors, the most important of which is probably the quality of the knowledgebase. Most resolvers come with a pre-populated knowledgebase from which a library can select their subscriptions. Others require that the library load the metadata for the knowledgebase themselves. Libraries should determine whether the electronic resources to which they would like to link are included in the knowledgebase. They should also ascertain whether they can easily load data into the knowledgebase themselves if a resource they need (such as local print holdings) is not covered. Some resolver vendors include more electronic journal and book providers in their knowledgebase than others, while some knowledgebases are more accurate than others.

Resolvers act as an intermediary between a patron and a resource that they want to acquire. Librarians should look carefully at the resolver's ability to introduce related information into the transaction. Some resolvers offer a high degree of visual customisability so that libraries can brand the resolver experience. Some allow the resolver to offer recommended links based on the metadata associated with a citation that the resolver is processing. For example, a resolver could offer links to biographical information about an author in a citation. Alternatively, a resolver could recognise the source of a citation as an anthropology database and suggest reference resources in anthropology.

Libraries wishing to purchase a resolver should also consider whether it is hosted locally or remotely. Because the data transferred to and from the resolver is a relatively small amount of text, there is no performance penalty in using a remotely hosted resolver. Furthermore, because resolvers are designed to work with remotely hosted resources, hosting a resolver locally does little to protect users from problematic Internet connections. The software and data on remotely hosted resolvers is normally updated automatically, following a more contemporary 'software as a service' approach.

Libraries with in-house database and web programming expertise may wish to develop their own resolver. By building a resolver in-house, a library has unlimited ability to customise the resolver while avoiding the purchase and maintenance fees associated with commercial products. Creating a knowledgebase is probably the most difficult part of constructing a resolver. However, the knowledgebase can be used for other purposes, such as providing a journal title search or customised reports for collection analysis.

Lewis & Clark College's Watzek Library and Willamette University's Hatfield Library have both developed their own OpenURL resolvers. Watzek Library constructed its resolver in 2003 when the commercial resolver market offered fewer affordable options. Their resolver consists of a relatively small PHP script that queries a multi-purpose print/ electronic journal database running on PostgreSQL. This script has been refined and customised to meet Watzek Library's needs better than available commercial options. Currently, PHP scripts load e-journal metadata provided by Serials Solutions and MARC holdings data from the library's Innovative Interfaces integrated library system (ILS) into the knowledgebase. This provides the resolver with full knowledge of print holdings information, a function difficult to find in a commercial resolver. The ILS loader script compares links found in the ILS with those from Serials Solutions and remove duplicates. This home-grown resolver has been extended with outbound linking options to an interlibrary loan form and to RefWorks bibliographic management software (Dahl, 2004).

While home-grown resolvers provide the ultimate customisability, commercial resolvers still have many opportunities to improve link services with customised programming and integration. For example, a library might create a script that takes the metadata from an outbound OpenURL and passes it on to a web application designed to record patron reviews about books, journal articles, etc.

One challenge facing the OpenURL model is that it depends on the information provider knowing which base URL to use when constructing OpenURLs. As a result, websites outside of digital libraries that link to articles (like most blogs, for instance) cannot use OpenURLs. Instead, they usually link to publisher websites, which often require a subscription or at least registration to access an article. In the case of books, the convention is to link to the record in Amazon. Ideally, patrons with access to subscription publications via a library to whom they are affiliated would be able to click on links to articles and be taken to a website that offers them free access to the article by virtue of their library affiliation.

The COinS (Context Objects in Spans) is a lightweight specification that attempts to solve this problem. Using COinS, someone composing a web page can embed the descriptor portion of an OpenURL within the HTML of the web page using 'span' tags that have metadata embedded in them. A browser extension can then translate those descriptors into links to an OpenURL link with a resolver designated by the patron (Hellman, 2005). In other words, COinS makes it possible to use the same link on a web page to direct people to subscription content through their regular library or information provider – even though they rely on different authentication mechanisms. COinS allows users to conveniently access journals and books referenced on the Web.

Digital object identifiers

A DOI is a series of characters that uniquely identifies digital content, such as a book or journal article. As such, its function is similar to that of ISBNs and UPC codes. For a DOI to be useful, it must be accessed using a DOI resolution service that maintains a centralised database along with the electronic address of the content itself or response page that provides appropriate information about the item and options for accessing it.

DOIs consist of a prefix and a suffix. Each issuing agency has its own prefix, and the suffix is a case-insensitive string of characters chosen by the issuing agency. All DOIs begin with 10, but neither the length of the suffix nor the prefix are limited. Furthermore, the format of the DOI is chosen by the issuing agency as the prefix ensures that different agencies cannot assign the same number. All DOIs created by an agency have the same prefix and but the prefix does not change if ownership of the resource is transferred to another agency.

DOIs are not required to have any meaning or contain check digits, though there is nothing to prevent the issuing agency from creating DOIs that are derived from meaningful values or which contain check digits. For example, if an agency were issued the prefix '23456' and wished to assign the suffix '1234567890ABCDEFG' to a resource, the resulting DOI would be: 10.123456/1234567890ABCDEFG.

Likewise, if the same agency wished to assign the DOI and the resource above was associated with ISBN 1-234567-89-X, the following would also be a perfectly legitimate DOI: 10.123456/ISBN1-234567-89-X.

Once a DOI has been assigned, it can be transmitted to a DOI resolution service to obtain the network address of the resource or other relevant information and services. It is important to be aware that DOIs do not replace OpenURLs or vice versa. Rather, they are complementary technologies that allow users to access a resource.

CrossRef is an organisation established by scholarly journal publishers that provides a DOI directory covering academically-oriented journals. Libraries can join CrossRef at no cost and utilise CrossRef's OpenURL-enabled directory to look up or submit DOIs. Practically speaking, CrossRef is the best way for an OpenURL resolver to link to an electronic journal article located at a journal publisher's website. A library's resolver simply needs to point an OpenURL for an article at CrossRef's OpenURL service and the patron who clicks on it will be forwarded to the article at the journal publisher's website.[2]

Federated searching

Federated searching, also known as 'metasearching', allows users to search multiple databases with a single query. Now that it is common for libraries to subscribe to dozens or even hundreds of research databases, users often do not know which database they need to search. Even when they know which databases may contain an item of interest, it is unreasonable for libraries to presume that users will learn dozens of search interfaces. For these reasons, federated searching systems are growing in popularity at libraries with large numbers of electronic resources.

In fact, the Z39.50 standard was originally created to provide a standardised way to search databases – in other words, to provide the infrastructure for a robust federated searching mechanism. Although Z39.50 is maintained by the Library of Congress, has major vendor support and is advocated by the library community, it has never achieved many of its goals. There are many reasons Z39.50 has failed, but the cost and complexity of implementing it have certainly undermined its implementation and the protocol is awkward to use in a web environment.

Federated searching has made great advances, but it has inherent limitations. Libraries subscribe to databases that contain different types of resources that are used for diverse purposes. Simultaneously querying divergent resources is inherently problematic.

Web search technology is very popular and people have great faith in it – a usability study at Northwestern University showed that users strongly prefer search-engine style results ranked by relevance, even if they have no idea how relevance is determined (Cervone, 2005). In many ways, libraries view federated searching as a means of bringing search-engine style searching to digital library resources like research databases.

Federated search engines must translate queries from a simplified search interface into the various query syntaxes native to the multiple resources that they are searching. Putting together a single, meaningful set of results from the search results provided by full-text databases, citation indexes, library catalogues, search engines, digital archives, etc. is technically and philosophically challenging. Methods for ranking relevance employed by popular search engines, such as Google and Yahoo do not translate well to federated searching. Major web search engines store information in their own databases and rank it according to their own criteria. By contrast, federated search engines translate user input to the native search syntax of databases developed by multiple vendors. These databases store data in a variety of structures that facilitate retrieval using a variety of algorithms. For this reason, federated searching systems cannot perform relevance ranking like search engines.

Furthermore, technical and legal constraints may prevent a library from using federated searching on important databases. Even when no such constraints exist, federated searching may cause undesirable side effects. For example, if the library can afford only one concurrent connection to an expensive technical database, an engineering professor might not be able to access it because a freshman rhetoric student is using the federated search engine to identify articles about smoking marijuana. By their very nature, federated searching products increase the frequency by which databases are searched – this complicates use analysis of individual databases for the purposes of electronic collection development and could prompt database vendors to raise prices.

At the time of writing, federated searching technology is still in its infancy and will most likely improve with time. A number of products are available on the market and they can be licensed through many ILS vendors as well as companies that specialise in federated searching. Locally hosted, as well as vendor hosted options are available. These products are differentiated by cost, which resources they can search, how they translate user input into the search syntax required for individual products and how they display the results retrieved.

Despite some of the challenges presented above, federated searching vendors have been advocating standards that would drastically simplify searching multiple databases. Of these standards, the most significant is SRU/W, a protocol that uses HTTP to execute sophisticated searches and retrieve the results in XML. SRU/W, HTTP and XML are discussed in Chapter 3.

It is possible that non-library standards, such as the Amazon-sponsored OpenSearch will prove more influential in the evolution of federated searching technology than library-based protocols, such as SRU/W and Z39.50. One of the challenges that Z39.50 and SRU/W face is that they are used almost exclusively by libraries, a very small part of the market. Consequently, developer and vendor interest is very low and few products support the standards. Consider, for example, the MARC format. Although it has played a central role in libraries for over 40 years, few tools exist that allow people to view or manipulate MARC records, and it still is virtually unheard of outside the library community. Although SRU/W is reasonably easy to implement, OpenSearch is even simpler and it returns the results in atom or RSS – which can easily be interpreted using a wide variety of popular software.

Content providers have already made databases containing news, music, images, video, products, jobs, library collections and other types of information available via OpenSearch. Anyone with access to the Web can already perform federated searches across hundreds of databases that support OpenSearch simply by going to an aggregator site, such as A9.com.[3] Rather than trying to convince content providers to support library protocols, federated searching may be achieved more effectively by embracing mainstream standards that already enjoy strong support.

Expanding role of search engines

Search engines play an increasingly important role in the delivery of digital library services. Users consult general and local web search engines to find, identify and locate services, as well as satisfy specific information needs. A 2005 report commissioned by OCLC established that most web users, including college students, in the UK, Canada, Australia,

USA and parts of Asia begin information searches with a search engine (De Rosa, 2005).

Because search engines allow users to access diverse services and resources from a single point, they have the effect of integrating services. As a greater proportion of the information users need can be identified with search engines and obtained over the Web, the distinctions between individual resources and services become blurred. As a result, users may not know which specific resources are appropriate for satisfying their information needs and they may not understand the purposes of individual resources or critical differences between them. For example, a student once remarked to one of the authors of this book that he did not like the catalogue because it was just a search engine that retrieved very little and did not actually let him see what he had found.

A few recent developments suggest that the role of search engines in digital library services will increase with time. First, commercial search engines now index an increasing amount of content that was formerly the domain of subscription library research databases. The websites of newspapers, magazines and scholarly journals commonly publish tables of contents and abstracts for back issues.

Reed Elsevier's Scirus search engine focuses on scientific websites and journal articles from freely available sources as well as subscription-based journals. Google Scholar specialises in indexing scholarly materials freely available on the Web, such as white papers in institutional repositories and articles in electronic journals. It also indexes citations found in those documents, further broadening its reach. Furthermore, Google has agreements with scholarly publishers and the CrossRef organisation to index content in subscription journals. Google has also incorporated the contents of OCLC's WorldCat catalogue into their index and includes items from this index in their Scholar results (Jascó, 2004).

Google Scholar has added the ability to link search results to an OpenURL resolver. This allows users to access books or articles in search results via their academic library's OpenURL resolver. Google Scholar has become a potential alternative to subscription research databases provided by academic libraries. Librarians have recognised this and for the most part embraced the opportunity to use the linking capability. Initial reviews of Google Scholar's searching capabilities have been mixed, however. At least in its beta phase, Scholar lacks the currency and searching flexibility of traditional subscription databases.[1]

Search engines like Google Scholar are a potential competitor to federated searching systems. In Scholar, Google has combined the types of content that academic libraries typically include in federated searching – full-text articles, citations and abstracts, book metadata – into a single index with a single search box. Because Scholar is a search engine, it retrieves results more quickly than federated searching and uses a single relevance ranking algorithm.

The success of Google's search model suggests that search engine technology may play a major role in the future of searching aggregated digital library content. However, the potential for commercial search engines to direct users to resources based on advertising revenue raises concerns about the effectiveness of them as research tools. Google Scholar's linking program, which does not allow libraries to use their own icon when linking to an OpenURL resolver, suggests that Google seeks to maintain more control over its interface than a typical library database vendor (Grogg, 2005).

One potential manifestation of search engine technology in digital libraries might be the establishment of firms that provide indexing or search services. A library would license a research database or full-text index from one firm, but pay for a third party to index the data along with other such data. The indexing firm would establish a relationship of trust with information vendors and the libraries so that all parties could be assured that their data would not be distributed inappropriately. Such a service would allow libraries to offer a search engine that covered premium content provided by various vendors as well as whatever local content they wanted exposed. Once users had located what they needed in the search service, they could be directed to the actual content via an OpenURL resolver. Although such services are not available at the time of writing this book, they seem a logical extension of the growing influence of search engine technology in libraries.

Some libraries, such as Bielefeld University Library in Germany, are actively developing search engine technology to use with their digital collections. Due to dissatisfaction with the functionality of federated searching products and wariness of the commercial focus of mainstream search engines, the Bielefeld University Library constructed its own search engine using technology from the Norwegian company Fast Search and Transfer (FAST). The Bielefeld Academic Search Engine (BASE) encompasses both metadata and full text from primarily non-commercial sources, especially institutional repositories. It harvests its data using the OAI protocol as well as traditional web crawling. The BASE approach reflects a belief that libraries need to take the initiative to build their own search engines collaboratively rather than rely on commercial vendors to do it. In two articles in *D-Lib Magazine*, Norbert Lossau expressed the vision of having commercial vendors provide data for the system with the incentive that their content will be better exposed. He envisions academically-oriented search engines that are restricted to academic content, handle multiple types of data objects, support advanced browsing and searching by various taxonomies and support flexible ranking and ordering schemes.[5]

The University of California Libraries (2005) report from its Taskforce on Bibliographic Services expresses a similar sentiment:

> In order to support a predictable federated search across a wide set of resources and to be able to build high-level searching and display services based on that search, a federated searching tool should pre-harvest as much metadata as possible. Google has shown the power of pre-harvesting metadata, applying sophisticated processing to the metadata and building a coherent set of services on top. We should create a similar set of services by pre-harvesting metadata for the full set of UC library collections.

The report envisions a search for a world leader that returns books, articles, conference papers and presentations, photographs and editorial cartoons about the leader as well as digitised letters that the leader wrote or received.

Another development in the search engine arena is the introduction of the Alexa Web Search Platform service from Amazon. Alexa effectively opens up the database of an Internet-wide search engine to programmers who can then develop specialised applications using the data and the search engine software. Under the Alexa model, a programmer can select a subset of the search engine's database and then query the database using Amazon's search software via a web services interface. Digital libraries might use this service or a similar one to build specialised search engines tailored to the subject focus of their library.[6]

A further involvement of commercial search engines into the digital library world is their recent interest in digitising print materials held in libraries. In late 2005 search engine companies embarked on two major digitisation projects. Google's Book Search project aims to digitise the public domain and copyrighted holdings of five major research libraries. This project's focus is on providing *searching* of the content of these digitised materials rather than the content itself, which would presumably be left to libraries and publishers (Price, 2004). The Open Content Alliance, a group that includes Yahoo, Microsoft and The Internet Archive as well as non-profit organisations, such as universities and archives, is focused on providing access to a broad repository of mostly public domain digitised content. The system for accessing and searching the content is yet unspecified but will be open enough for individual organisations to create specialised search engines to search subsets of its content (Price, 2005).

Many applications of search engine technology are hard to implement in small to medium-sized libraries. Digital library integrators should seek to include search engines applicable to the focus of their library in their portals, and localise those search engines with OpenURLs if possible. As opportunities arise for smaller scale operators to customise large search engines like Amazon's Alexa and that of the Open Content Alliance, digital libraries will be able to harness the power of search engines and make them a central part of their digital library portal.

Locally developed integration

Opportunities for integrating vendor-supplied content into a digital library exist beyond the frameworks described above. Examples of such integration include:

- a system that checks a potential interlibrary loan request against several sources – including a union catalogue and a database of electronic serials – before passing through the request;

- an electronic reserves system that deep links to electronic articles on journal publishers' websites;

- a web application that adds table of contents data to an OPAC using RSS feeds from journal publishers' websites;

- a web application that inserts book reviews into an OPAC using Amazon's web services API;

- an extension to an OpenURL resolver that exports citation metadata to RefWorks bibliographic management software.

Developing effective local solutions usually takes some programming expertise with the kinds of web scripting technologies described in Chapter 2. When making systems work together, the greatest challenge is typically to get external content providers to share information in a way that a web application can process. The techniques for connecting to external content providers fall along the same lines as those for connecting to an ILS:

- special programs that interact with interfaces designed for users (also referred to as 'screen scraping');

- application programming interfaces (APIs);

- standards-based APIs or protocols, such as OpenURL, SRU/W, Z39.50, etc.

Screen scraping is the slowest, least reliable and most difficult method for automating communication between systems. In the web environment, it translates into processing HTML designed to be browsed by humans. Programs that use this method are sometimes hard to maintain and prone to failure because web interfaces change without notice. However, sometimes there is no other viable option.

APIs are standardised interfaces that content providers offer that allow external programmers to access their data and functionality. Amazon offers an API that permits access to the data in their vast catalogue, including book metadata and consumer reviews of products; Wikipedia also offers an API with access to its contents. Time and programming skills are necessary to take advantage of an API, and unless they conform to a standard, work done to interface with one vendor's API will not work with another's.

Standardised protocols, such as OpenURL, SRU/W and RSS are the best way of connecting with content providers. Some standardised protocols like RSS and OpenSearch are widely implemented inside and outside of the library community. However, at the time of writing, many standardised protocols, such as SRU/W and COinS do not have widespread support even among library content providers, much less content providers outside the library world.

Fortunately, digital library integrators can use any of these techniques with scripting languages that have strong text processing capabilities like PHP and Perl. Depending on the application, the logic involved might need to be quite detailed, so actually achieving integration can take some time.

Digital library integrators should not hesitate to mash content from various information providers to improve services or create new ones. Many possibilities for new applications and services exist. For example, by leveraging OpenURLs and some HTML screen scraping, Oregon State University developed a system that checks incoming interlibrary loan requests against readily available print and electronic resources.

Many libraries are now incorporating external content into their digital library through APIs and web standards like RSS. Furthermore, OpenURLs and DOIs have made it possible to deep link to resources from many contexts besides the OpenURL resolver, including electronic reserve systems, citation management systems and social bookmarking software.

Summary

- Technologies used to integrate content fit into two basic groups – those which permit 'deep linking' to retrieve known items and those that search multiple resources simultaneously for unknown items.

- OpenURL is a very simple but widely supported protocol that is useful for linking citations to full text or automatically creating interlibrary loan requests.

- Libraries that are purchasing an OpenURL resolver should consider several factors when shopping for a resolver: cost, hosting, knowledgebase scope and quality, and configurability of the knowledgebase, user interface and resolver behaviour.

- COinS is an emerging, ad hoc protocol for including OpenURL descriptors in web pages so that the OpenURL can be used with a resolver identified by the user rather than the website providing the URL.

- DOIs are useful for identifying electronic content. However, like OpenURL, they must be used with a resolution service to connect users directly to content.

- Federated searching allows users to search multiple databases with a single query. While they are convenient to use, a number of practical issues prevent federated search engines from working as effectively as popular general web search engines. However, federated searching technology is still developing rapidly and is expected to improve.

- Search engines have the effect of integrating services because they allow users to access diverse services and resources from a single point. However, they also make it more difficult for users to distinguish between different kinds of resources.

- Commerical search engines, such as Google Scholar now search some of the same type of content traditionally found in subscription-based electronic indexes purchased by libraries.

- In the academic library community, there is some interest in using search engines to search across a large body of harvested content traditionally held in separate information silos, such as library catalogues, research databases, institutional repositories and image databases.

- Because libraries support very diverse missions and resources, a moderate amount of local programming expertise is usually required to achieve significant integration with content providers.

- 'Screen scraping', APIs, are popular tools for integrating digital library services with content providers.

Notes

1 OpenURLs also work using the HTTP POST method.
2 See: *http://www.crossref.org/* (accessed: 12 January 2006).
3 See: *http://opensearch.a9.com/* (accessed: 17 February 2006).
4 For a good overview of Google Scholar's program for libraries see Grogg (2005). For a review of Google Scholar's search performance in social science literature, see Gardner and Eng (2005).
5 See: *http://base.ub.uni-bielefeld.de/index_english.html* (accessed: 14. January 2006). Two articles on the BASE concept are Loussau (2004) and Summann (2004).
6 See: *http://websearch.alexa.com* (accessed: 15 January 2006).

9

Library portals

The library portal is the culmination of digital library integration. To succeed, it must combine a wide variety of information and services into a single user interface. Multiple information services within the library and the parent organisation must work in concert to achieve this result. The ultimate goal of this integration effort is meeting the needs of users in a networked environment. Various ways that a library portal can achieve this goal are discussed below. This chapter is also concerned with the skill sets needed to achieve success.

Covered in this chapter:

- a provisional definition of portal types;

- the nature of different portal strategies;

- the skills required for successful portal development;

- the portal as information hub and as distributed network services.

What is a library portal?

Because the meaning of the term may not be obvious, we need to begin by answering the question: what is a library portal? This book has already provided one answer: a library portal is the culmination of digital library integration. Admittedly, however, this isn't very helpful. It's like saying that a picture is what you see when all the dots are connected. Yes, but a picture of what?

To some extent, the answer varies from library to library. We began this book by discussing the earliest library websites. These sites were composed of static web pages, with links to the library catalogue, databases and websites of interest. At many small libraries today, when you connect the dots that make up the library portal, this is more or less what you see.

At larger libraries, the portal picture is considerably more complicated and rapidly evolving. In these settings, dozens of technologies and standards described in this book may be at work behind the scenes. When you connect these dots, the picture that emerges might be a harmonious composition or a work in multiple, interrelated panels. It might seem pleasing and accessible to some, yet quite possibly complicated and difficult to others.

To push the metaphor just a little further, what if the dots create a sculpture in three dimensions, with front, back and sides? A viewer who approaches the sculpture from one direction will see something quite different from another viewer on the opposite side of the room. Is a library portal like a sculpture with many possible views? Or like a picture with one angle of approach?

We assume that a library portal can in fact be like any of the above. It can be a simple website made up largely of links to library content and services; it can be a complex website composed of many carefully integrated services; and it can be an integrated bundle of services accessed from many different points in the networked environment. For the sake of discussion, we will call these simple, well-integrated and well-rounded portals.

The simple portal

At its simplest level, a library portal begins with a well-designed website that provides links to library resources. These resources might include the online catalogue, other library catalogues, union catalogues, networked databases and full-text sources. Integration is achieved largely by linking to these and other services from the library homepage. The library catalogue, interlibrary loan system, electronic reserves and other services are independent and accessed separately by the user. They may, however, be partially integrated through similar web page layout, graphic design and a consistent navigation scheme.

Because no amount of programming finesse can overcome the shortcomings of a poorly organised user interface, all library portals require good web design. The creation of portal interfaces begins with information architecture, navigation schemes and graphic design. Forming a design team, negotiating the constraints of the library or parent organisation's design policies, developing organisation and labelling strategies and conducting usability tests all require major investments of time and energy that cannot be glossed over, even in a book that is focused on the more technical aspects of digital libraries.

Most library websites also facilitate browsing electronic databases alphabetically or by subject. In medium to large-sized libraries, this list of resources can be quite long. Given the number of resources involved, many libraries use the scripting languages and relational database systems described in Chapter 2 to dynamically generate web pages for these resources. This technique additionally allows library staff to maintain content by entering information into a form rather than by directly editing web pages. Other portions of the library's web presence can be managed in a similar way, thus allowing numerous staff to participate in the maintenance of library content without mastering the intricacies of HTML. As necessary, staff might also use the authoring and site maintenance capabilities of a desktop tool like Dreamweaver to manage other portions of the site.

Many libraries purchase online information about their electronic journal subscriptions from a publication access management service (PAMS). PAMS are described further in Chapter 6. These services typically provide A–Z lists and journal search tools that are hosted on the vendor site. Libraries can, however, add their own branding and navigation features to this remotely hosted content, effectively integrating these services into the library's own portal framework. Libraries might also purchase the OpenURL link resolver services discussed in Chapter 8 from a PAMS or other service provider, and configure these services to match the library's portal design.

A proxy service can be an essential feature of a simple library portal. Proxy services allow access to IP restricted content from locations outside the parent organisation's network domain. Access to a proxy service requires password authentication and authorisation (Chapter 3). Within a simple portal framework, access to services like proxy servers, patron circulation records, interlibrary loan and electronic reserves will typically require separate logins by the user.

In some library settings, library portals are implemented using a commercial content management system (CMS) supported by the library or the parent organisation. Content management systems provide tools for submitting content, managing workflow and approval, and implementing highly consistent CSS and template driven designs. Libraries often find that some of their content and services cannot be delivered effectively using a commercial CMS system. Yet where it makes sense, these systems can be useful ways to develop a consistent web presence.

Many libraries have also begun to incorporate blog software into their websites, primarily as a way to announce and syndicate library news and events. One optional feature of blog applications is the opportunity for users to post comments. A properly managed blog may be used as a public forum for feedback about library services or events.

Virtual reference is also possible in relatively simple library portals, thanks to reference-oriented chat applications or instant messaging services. Instant messaging is the simplest and most direct approach to providing online reference. By providing a link to instructions on how to connect to library instant messaging accounts, establishing these accounts on widely used instant messaging services like Yahoo, and giving librarians the necessary chat software, it is relatively easy to extend personal library support to individuals working remotely.

All of these services fit the model of a simple web portal that utilises generic web technologies and relatively modest programming skills. It reasonable to assume that most libraries today support some or all of the following in their portal environment:

- clearly organised presentation of library services that facilitates both research and library instruction;

- content management tools and dynamic web pages where appropriate;

- proxy services for access to licensed content;

- OpenURL resolution services;

- access to all library services through separate access paths and logins.

The role of the digital library integrator in this setting requires a number of skills. These include HTML, CSS, JavaScript, web server administration, scripting and relational database abilities, knowledge of library technologies, such as the ILS and interlibrary loan systems, knowledge of operating systems and an understanding of network protocols like DNS, HTTP and LDAP.

The well-integrated portal

As one might expect, the complicated picture is less easy to describe. A more advanced portal shares many qualities with its modest counterpart.

Good web design, dynamically driven web pages, authoring tools and content management systems, either commercial or locally developed, carry over into any portal context. Advanced portal development, however, seeks a higher level of integration and more powerful tools for information discovery.

The chief goal of a well-integrated portal is to overcome the fragmentation of information and services that is the status quo of simple library portals. Achieving this goal requires more sophisticated technologies. Wikipedia defines web portals as:

> ... sites on the World Wide Web that typically provide personalised capabilities to their visitors. They are designed to use distributed applications, different numbers and types of middleware and hardware to provide services from a number of different sources.

The term 'middleware' in this definition refers largely to the database management systems, scripting technologies, CGI applications and web services that are described elsewhere in this book.

The LibPortal Project undertaken by Loughborough University (LISU, 2004) further extends our thinking by describing a portal as:

> ... a network service that brings together content from diverse distributed resources using technologies, such as cross-searching, harvesting and alerting and collates this into an amalgamated form for presentation to the user.

As in the Wikipedia definition, the LibPortal report envisions a variety of distributed applications presented seamlessly to the user via single user interface. Yet by emphasising the role that portals play in information discovery, the LibPortal definition adds library-specific components to the earlier definition.

Cross-searching – otherwise known as federated searching – and aggregation via metadata harvesting are strategies for simplifying the information discovery process. Federated searching passes a single query to multiple information sources and presents search results to the user in a single, integrated interface. Aggregation, by contrast, harvests metadata from multiple repositories and provides a single search of this combined information. These strategies can in practice be combined by searching across multiple sets of previously harvested and aggregated data. Facilitating information discovery by either method attempts to achieve a very ambitious goal: that of making basic library research as simple and effective as using an Internet search engine like Google.

By including federated searching and aggregation (via harvesting) in its definition of a portal, the LibPortal report invites us to think ambitiously about what a library portal might accomplish. Rather than navigate library catalogues, proprietary databases, institutional or cross-disciplinary repositories, blogs and other services, the user can begin the discovery process through a single search. The ability to view and evaluate search results from multiple sources within a uniform interface aids the research process and meets increasing user expectations for easy information access.

Federated searching not surprisingly raises debates within the library profession about the 'dumbing-down' of research, as well as the trade-off between teaching users to select and use native proprietary interfaces on the one hand, and meeting expectations for Google-like ease of use on the other. This debate is fuelled in part by the inherent weaknesses of federated search technology. As of writing, commercial products that offer federated searching include MetaLib, from Ex Libris, WebFeat and MuseGlobal. A number of open source federated search initiatives are also underway. All of these solutions, however, share a number of common flaws. For example, it is currently impossible for federated search tools to truly de-dupe search results or apply the kind of relevancy ranking that is possible for a search engine like Google.

Aggregation strategies offer hope for better results. For this reason, pre-harvesting data is a strategy favoured by many, including the University of California Libraries Taskforce on Bibliographic Services (2005) report, which argues that 'a federated search tool should pre-harvest as much metadata as possible'. Providing useful access to pre-harvested metadata from bibliographic databases, catalogues and repositories requires the kind of metadata translation activities discussed in Chapter 7, as well as knowledge of metadata formats described in Chapter 3. This can add considerably to the skill set required of digital library integrators.

Looking toward the future, Semantic Web technology may contribute to better federated searching. For example, the SIMILE project, a joint undertaking of the W3C, MIT Libraries and MIT Computer Science and Artificial Intelligence Laboratory (CSAIL), attempts to apply Semantic Web concepts to the problem of searching across arbitrary metadata schema (Mazzocchi et al., 2005). Metadata aggregation and cross-thesaurus mapping via semantic technologies may in the long run provide a rich vocabulary for federated searching across diverse content domains and systems. To the degree that this Semantic Web capability is achieved and implemented in disciplinary databases and repository systems, we are likely to see significant improvement in federated search capabilities.

Another modest and less scaleable approach to semantic interoperability also has an impact on portal services. Making the library portal 'aware' of the information contained in a parent organisation's enterprise system can facilitate meaningful personalised services. Consider the case of course enrolment information or information about an individual's status as a student, faculty or staff member. If, after a secure login, the portal service knows this information, it can offer personalised features like electronic reserves or library services offered specifically to faculty.

In many settings, this integration with enterprise systems can be difficult to achieve. In the best of circumstances, a portal application will obtain user information through web services or APIs that facilitate live communication with the enterprise system. When this is not possible, the digital library integrator may work with IT staff to create a mechanism for exporting selected user information from the enterprise system into an external service, like an LDAP directory (Chapter 4). The knowledge and skill required to work effectively with IT staff outside the library thus becomes an important aspect of effective library portal development.

Yet another component of back-end integration is discussed in Chapter 6. Electronic resource management systems (ERMS) offer tools that help libraries manage many of the activities related to the acquisition and use of licensed information resources. Management information provided by an ERM solution can include resource descriptions, coverage data and licence terms. An ERMS may also facilitate the management of proxy services that are a critical component of content delivery. ERM services should ideally function as an integral part of the library portal.

Syndication and alerting services are another portal feature growing in popularity. RSS feeds from news services, blogs and other sources are a way for individuals to stay abreast of developments in areas of personal or professional interest. Such services also make sense in a library setting. In the past, libraries have provided faculty with table of contents alerting services. Library portals can take these services a step further by providing, for example, alerts to new library acquisitions that match a user's area of research or to additions to local or remote repository collections.

The well-integrated library portal also solves the annoying problem of separate logins to library services distributed across multiple systems. Single sign on (SSO) for access to account information, circulation records, the status of interlibrary loan requests, materials on reserve for a course and other services is achieved through authentication and authorisation services that bind a particular user session to all of these services. Some of the difficulties inherent in creating a single login for library services are discussed in Chapter 4.

The well-integrated library portal is thus a comprehensive user interface that integrates many distributed applications into a single, personalised user service that overcomes the fragmented digital library landscape through such features as:

- federated search tools that simplify the process of discovery;

- complete library account information accessed through SSO;

- intelligent presentation of services based on a user's status or profile;

- personalised syndication and alerting services;

- integration with back-end library and enterprise-wide systems.

The skills required to achieve this well-integrated portal build on those already required for developing a simple library portal. They include advanced skills in scripting and applications development, LDAP, network security, XML and XSLT data translation, metadata formats, web services and APIs. As libraries move toward a more complex portal interface, digital library integrators must work closely with IT staff, metadata specialists and public service librarians. Evaluation of vendor and open source solutions must be informed by the goals of the library and the technical resources available in the wider campus environment.

The well-rounded portal

Up to this point we have considered the portal as a comprehensive hub for library services. This implicitly assumes that online researchers will or should approach the library portal as their comprehensive gateway to information, much as a picture or painting is approached and taken in from a single vantage point. Yet is the networked environment really like this? Do users always 'come to the library' first, and, for that matter, should they?

Lorcan Dempsey (2003) has argued that the concept of library portals as information hubs is problematic:

It is often imagined that the 'portal' answers the question of how the library fruitfully engages the variety of resources and the variety of user needs. At best, however, I argue, the portal is only a partial answer; at worst, it obscures the real question.

Dempsey points to the existence of other network services in the academic environment. A course management system (CMS) creates information hubs for the classes in which a student is enrolled. Campus or organisational portals create yet another information access point with a more general audience. Potential library users will surely find other information or community hubs that address their needs or interests. As Dempsey points out, it is not possible for all of these locations to be one-stop shops. 'In short, a portal – however defined – is not a substitute for a strategy of effective use and management of resources in a network environment; it is a part of it'.

The well-rounded portal is part of a more general strategy to meet user needs in the networked environment. To return one last time to our metaphor, it is like a sculpture in its surrounding environment. Person A sees something quite different from Person B, depending on where they stand in relation to it. Thus, a library service incorporated into a CMS is one view. That same library service incorporated into the university portal is another view. There is, of course, the straight-on view, in which we see the plenitude of the integrated library portal as described in the previous section. Like our statue in the round, however, each view is generated by the same underlying service.

One inevitable characteristic of the well-rounded portal is modularity. It should be possible to decouple library services from each other, as well as separate underlying content from its presentation. A library that has implemented a 'my account' feature within its integrated portal might wish to offer this same account information to a student who has logged into a university portal. If the library account feature is implemented as a web service through which account information can be gathered and exported in a known XML schema, the same service can be used simultaneously by the integrated library portal and the university portal. Library account information is thus visible in two distinct contexts and functions in a way analogous to a sculpture seen from multiple vantage points.

Examples of this portal strategy are fairly common, although the implementation techniques will vary. Librarians and IT staff at the University of Nebraska have, for example, developed an automated connection between the Blackboard CMS and the library's electronic reserve system. The ability to search learning repositories like MERLOT or search engines like Google from within a Blackboard CMS may be extended to other repositories. The RSS newsfeeds feature supported by many CMS and campus portals can be used with syndicated library information. Open source CMS and campus portal projects (Moodle and uPortal, for example) promise even greater opportunities for integration. At least one ILS vendor now supports the ability to integrate with uPortal using 'channel' technology (Breeding, 2005).

Developing the well-rounded portal is not an exclusive library activity. Integration into a wider environment will often require collaboration and joint planning. At most institutions, however, the wagon for selecting CMS and campus-wide portals is not being pulled by the library pony. The library may need to actively pursue involvement in these software decisions and earn credibility through informed participation. This strategic planning role is one of the important contributions made by enterprising digital library integrators.

Web 2.0 and the portal

A new generation of web applications characterised by social computing, data sharing and relatively easy-to-use APIs for moving information between applications (usually referred to as data 'mashing') have been collectively characterised as the next generation of web computing or Web 2.0. It may be only a matter of time before we forget the label, but many of the applications being developed are significant and will have a lasting effect on libraries as they develop new strategies for the networked future. We'd like to cite just one example of how the well-rounded portal might become a part of the Web 2.0 scene.

Social bookmarking services are one of the success stories in the social computing world. These services do two fundamental things. They allow individuals to easily store bookmarked web resources on the bookmarking service's site. These bookmarks are available both to the individual and to other users of the service. Second, these services allow the user to 'tag' their bookmarks for organisational purposes. The tags that a user creates for their bookmarks are also shared with other users of the service.

These user-defined tags are a personal taxonomy. And because the members of a social bookmarking service can see the tags and bookmarks of others, a natural process of information sharing unfolds. Users begin to mine each other's links, build similar collections and organise their ideas around similar concepts. The tags within the bookmarking service take on the characteristics of what has come to be called a 'folksonomy', or a taxonomy developed by the collective intelligence of users.

The communities of discourse that build these folksonomies can be powerful tools for research. How libraries might add value to this process becomes an intriguing question. One possible answer is to build a bridge between the folksonomy and the library's own metadata services.

For example, a bookmarking service like Connotea has well-developed OpenURL capabilities that allow bookmarks to be configured for access to a library's OpenURL resolver. The library's resolver service in turn provides deep links to resources owned by the library.

What if the library's resolver knowledgebase includes subject headings that have been assigned to the requested journal title? It might then be possible to provide extended services via the link resolver. Related journal titles or a subject-limited federated search of related databases might be offered to the user. If the Connotea user discovers new resources in the process of following these suggested research paths, these resources could be bookmarked and added to the Connotea service.

In effect, the service above uses an incoming OpenURL request to generate context-aware mini-portal services. The user moves from a resource initially found in the folksonomy of a bookmarking service, into a subject-driven recommendation service provided by the library and adds any references found back into the shared folksonomy. This scenario illustrates how a well-rounded portal service might be creatively integrated into emerging network practices. Admittedly hypothetical and untested, it nevertheless provides a possible example of the well-rounded portal in action.

The well-rounded library portal thus adds the following features to our list of possible portal characteristics:

- modular features that can be repackaged for use in other portal contexts, like course management systems;

- context-aware portal services;

- graceful integration into a variety of user workflows and research paths.

Developing theses services will require a well-rounded digital library integrator. Creativity, an awareness of emerging technologies, an ability to work well with others and an enterprising approach to addressing digital library challenges will be required.

Final considerations

Portal development is of immediate and strategic importance to a library. Its goal is meeting the needs of users in a specific networked environment.

This development takes place in dynamic and changing technological context. A central claim of this book is that the technologies needed to develop sophisticated end-user services are now ubiquitous and accessible. These technologies give libraries flexibility and control that would have been unobtainable in an earlier era of computing. Developments in web computing make it realistic for libraries to 'glue' applications together in meaningful and reliable ways that enhance service delivery. At the same time, the library and open source communities are building tools that drive such innovative developments as digital repositories, OpenURL link resolvers and new information protocols that facilitate research and discovery. Library technology vendors are incorporating these technologies into their own products.

Library portals can thus be implemented in many ways. At least one library automation vendor offers an integrated portal service that claims to be a true one-stop interface for all library needs. One must ask, however, whether this glistening new information hub has increasingly little to do with how research is actually done in a networked environment? Perhaps this question can only be answered in light of local circumstances and local needs. Any given product or assembly of products, may be the right fit for an organisation. The key point to remember is this: the library portal is not the strategy; it is a part of the strategy. One of the essential roles of digital library integrators is to help their colleagues – inside and outside the library organisation – choose and implement the right strategy to improve library service. Playing this role requires the kind of skills and knowledge outlined in this book.

Summary

- The library portal exists to meet the networked information needs of users.

- Users may rely on more than one information hub to support their research.

- Integration is the key to meeting information needs. Two types of integration are of primary importance to portal development: integration that overcomes the fragmentation of library information and services, and integration into the workflow of networked information users.

- Increasing complex digital library opportunities require the skills of competent digital library integrators who can help map an effective strategy for a library or institution.

10

Conclusion: digital libraries and the library organisation

This book has demonstrated that libraries operate in a very heterogeneous content and systems environment. It has explored the technologies available to bind together resources and services to create a more effective information seeking environment for library users. It has not, however, explored the organisational implications of constructing and maintaining a digital library. This chapter will discuss how digital libraries fit into the organisational structure of a library. It will review the qualities needed in the staff that support a digital library. It will discuss the crucial implications that a digital library has on strategic planning for the library and its parent organisation. Finally, it will conclude with some thoughts on the future of digital library integration.

Covered in this chapter:

- organisational structure and digital libraries;

- knowledge and skills needed by library staff;

- strategic planning;

- the future of digital library integration.

Digital library development and the library organisation

Ideally, digital library integration work should be tightly woven into the fabric of any modern library organisation. It should touch on almost all aspects of what a library does. For our analytical purposes, however, digital library integration work fits into the organisational structure of a library in three major ways:

- technical (or 'systems') personnel devoted to installing, configuring and developing digital library systems;

- personnel in other areas of the library whose work supports the digital library;

- cross-functional teams that encompass both types of personnel.

Where do the personnel that do the technical aspect of digital library work fit into a library organisation? A central systems or automation division is the most traditional place. Whether staffed by a single systems librarian or by several personnel, a systems division can provide a broad base of support for a library's technical needs. These might include microcomputer and server support, ILS upgrades and maintenance, and digital library applications.[1]

The model of a systems librarian still works well for some libraries. Increasingly, however, libraries are creating special positions and in some cases, special organisational units to address digital library integration needs. These types of positions have titles, such as 'digital services coordinator', 'digital access librarian', etc. These types of departments have names, such as the University of Nevada-Las Vegas's 'Web and Digitisation Services' division or Victoria University of New Zealand's 'Digital Services' department. Sometimes these departments emphasise digital library development that directly benefits patron research and report to the head of public services. In other cases, their work focuses on managing a library's virtual collections and they report to the head of collection management. Elsewhere, they focus on both areas and report to the library director.

In larger libraries, separate systems or information technology divisions often remain to handle the basic technology infrastructure of the library. In smaller libraries, this infrastructure support is often outsourced to the parent institution's IT department. The separation of IT infrastructure support from digital library development reflects the differing priorities, values and skills needed to fulfil these two functions. As Nicholas G. Carr (2004) points out in his book, *Does IT Matter?*, much information technology infrastructure is a commodity shared by all organisations. Digital library integration work, by contrast, is a core competency unique to the business of libraries.

The new organisational units focusing on digital services reflect the increasing importance of technologies higher up the 'stack' (in the areas of web applications, relational databases, etc.). They tend to emphasise experimentation and customised services. By contrast, IT professionals supporting infrastructure tend to emphasise stability and upgrading to the latest standardised technology. Because the very nature of digital library work is so experimental and encourages customised work, the culture of the digital library integrator can clash with that of the more conservatively oriented information technology manager. Library leaders should strive for a harmonious, cooperative relationship between information technology and digital library units in their organisation. They should also recognise that these units often have different goals and priorities.

Public services

Traditionally, library public services encompass reference, instruction and access services (circulation, reserves, interlibrary loan). Public services personnel support library patrons as they use library services. With the rise of the Internet and digital libraries, public services librarians have begun to think differently about how they provide that support. In earlier times, much of their interaction with the public was devoted to guiding patrons through the mechanics of searching the online catalogue or reference indexes. Patrons have become accustomed to accessing digital libraries remotely and request less personal assistance than they did a few years ago. Consequently, traditional reference desk enquiries have dropped at most academic libraries. Even though reference service through non-traditional means, such as e-mail and chat shows promise, public services librarians are struggling to figure out their role in this new environment.

Some librarians view the teaching of information literacy skills as an essential role for librarians in higher education. Information literacy encompasses a range of skills required to navigate the digital information environment. It can be an important means of drawing students into the digital library and helping them use it to the fullest extent. Those librarians teaching information literacy need a strong grasp of digital technologies employed in academic digital libraries as well as the Web as a whole.

Librarians are increasingly using web-based tools to assist patrons. For example, reference librarians often refer patrons to entries in Ullrich's periodical directory to discover which research databases index which periodical. In the past, such a referral was something that usually happened in a reference interview. Now, however, reference librarians can tune a link resolver to make the referral automatically as a patron looks up a journal in an online catalogue. In a similar vein, a librarian may have manually compiled special lists of resources or 'bibliographies' for patrons in the past. Now, they might design an online database that allows patrons to build such lists in a self-service fashion.

As the Web becomes increasingly essential to provision of services, public services librarians will need to participate actively in the design, construction, evaluation and promotion of digital library services. They will be required to play an active, if not leading, role in developing and configuring digital library systems, such as web portals, OPACs, federated searching systems, link resolvers and digital collections systems. They will be expected to become proficient at analysing the statistics provided by various digital library components. They will need to organise and run usability tests, mount surveys and employ focus groups to evaluate their digital libraries. And they will need to be able to oversee changes to their digital library systems based on the results of the information that they gather.

Academic librarians are also beginning to develop collaborative relationships with teaching faculty on specific projects. These projects might include developing a research assignment for a class or partnering with a professor to support student thesis work. Key to the notion of faculty–librarian collaboration is that librarians bring unique information management skills to the table. In the digital library environment, these skills could include the construction of websites, specialised databases and citation sharing tools. Librarians who are able to wield the full power of their digital library will be the ones with whom faculty will be interested in collaborating.[2]

Collection management and special collections

A library's collection management (or 'technical services') department is traditionally responsible for the back-room processing of the library's collection. They order, physically process and catalogue books and serials. In the digital library environment, they are increasingly responsible for ordering and tracking electronic products, especially electronic journals. They are also often responsible for adding metadata to local digital collections.

As digital library integration improves and as the proportion of a library's content that is digital increases, collection management departments in most libraries should require fewer staff. More advanced and integrated electronic tools should allow a small number of staff to manage many electronic journal subscriptions. The work of physically processing print journals and eventually print books should decrease as those media gradually go out of favour. And even for the print content that lingers, more automated processing should reduce the need for staff.

Two major roles for library collection management departments will emerge in the future. Metadata management librarians will oversee the manipulation of aggregated metadata for non-unique electronic collections. They will also catalogue unique materials using appropriate taxonomies, such as MODS and EAD. Collection management staff will use electronic resource management systems to acquire and track an increasing number of licensed electronic resources and integrate them into the digital library.

Library special collections, archives and rare book departments are often highly involved in the development of local digital collections and will continue to be in the future. Much of the day-to-day work of archivists and special collections librarians will involve digital collection planning and grant writing, the creation of digital finding aids and the design of digital preservation strategies. Especially in larger libraries, these types of departments will employ technical digital production staff to develop digitisation workflows and work out the complex technical issues of creating digital collections.

Cross-functional teams

Because digital library integration work touches most areas of library operations, library leaders have often addressed it by creating cross-functional teams that can work together to design systems and solve problems. These teams often transcend traditional organisational boundaries and departments, and are often led by an individual without authority over the team members. For example, an electronic resources management team might consist of a systems librarian, a reference librarian, an acquisitions librarian and a serials specialist. Similarly, a 'web design' team might consist of an instruction librarian, an electronic resources librarian, a digital services librarian and a web designer from the parent institution's public relations department.

Cross-functional teams work well for projects that cross organisational boundaries and involve technical and non-technical staff. They are an excellent way to leverage the expertise of individuals across an organisation, including staff from outside the library department. Library managers must be careful, however, to understand the limits of the less formal team approach in the delivery of digital library services. Teams that attempt to distribute specialised, technical work like web development across a group of employees without the time, training or focus to get the job done right are likely to fail.

At the University of Texas Southwestern Medical Center at Dallas Library, an analysis of their current organisational structure revealed that some of their voluntary, cross-functional teams were collapsing under the weight of expanding duties. For example, their Virtual Library Team was responsible for the content and design of their website. As team duties increased with the size and scope of the library's site, it became difficult for staff members to properly prioritise their team work with the regular duties written in their job descriptions. A subsequent organisational restructure formalised much of the Virtual Library Team's work in a new Digital Access Department (Higa, 2005).

As a library's content becomes more digital and as the systems needed to support the digital library grow, it may be necessary to make changes to a library's formal organisational structure. A digital services department devoted to developing and maintaining web-based library services might be one such change. Developing new non-technical positions that support digital library services may also be necessary. Such positions could include electronic resource management librarian, distance education services librarian, metadata management librarian and electronic serials management specialist.

Skills for digital library personnel

The most crucial element to developing a successful digital library is having the right staff in place. Libraries are often very stable organisations with limited staff turnover and limited resources to add additional staff. For these reasons, library directors may find it difficult to adjust their staffing to meet digital library needs.

Specialised technology staff offer the most direct way of addressing digital library integration needs. The traditional systems librarian has a Master of Library and/or Information Science (MLIS) degree and some supplemental training and/or experience in computer and information systems. The training in information management provided by an MLIS is often helpful when developing digital library services. In addition, many recent MLIS programmes provide training that is highly relevant to digital library integration work. A recent listing of courses available at the University of Washington Information School included 'Conceptual Database Design', 'Programming for Information Systems', and 'Internet Technologies and Applications'.[3]

Many of the skills needed for digital library integration, including web scripting, relational database management and web design, are also possessed by candidates without an MLIS. Bringing in new talent with a perspective from outside the library profession can breathe new energy and ideas into a library's digital initiatives.

Perhaps the greatest barrier to hiring the appropriate technical staff in small to medium-sized libraries is a lack of tradition in doing so. Often, the systems librarian in a small library will only have experience purchasing and configuring vendor-supplied products. The library director will have little experience hiring and supervising staff whose job it is to build and customise web applications. Furthermore, the parent institution's information technology department may discourage the library from pursuing technology initiatives on their own. Library managers in this predicament should seek guidance outside their organisation to help develop a strategy for acquiring the technical expertise that they need.

Building a wider library staff with broad-based integration skills is perhaps a greater challenge than hiring staff dedicated to working out digital library problems. Roy Tennant of the California Digital Library has identified a set of desirable characteristics for digital librarians. Indeed, these characteristics are desirable for anyone working in a modern library environment. They include flexibility, scepticism about new developments in technology, the willingness to take risks, a public service perspective, a team-oriented approach, the ability to lead change and the ability to work independently. He argues, correctly, that these characteristics should trump specific skills in particular information technologies when evaluating applicants (Tennant, 2004).

It is neither possible nor desirable for every individual in a library to be a technical expert. But individuals in all areas of information services need to develop an aptitude for leveraging technology to solve problems and improve services. Ideally, library staff, whether they are in serials management, library instruction or another area of library work, should have an eye for the possibilities of technology and should seek to make those possibilities a reality. They need to learn a way of thinking that is capable of approaching information management problems within the basic framework of the Web. This includes an understanding of basic web technologies like web pages, blogs and wikis. It also requires adoption of the basic conventions of communication on the Web, such as hyperlinking a particular word in a body of text as a way of connecting together documents.

A report from the National Research Council (1999) describes a type of aptitude known as 'fluency in information technology' that is a prerequisite for this kind of employee. The report contends that many individuals can use applications on computers but do not have an understanding of the underlying concepts of information technology and computing. If they did, their ability to learn new systems and apply existing systems to problems would increase dramatically.

The intellectual capabilities that the report advocates are all highly relevant to solving digital library integration problems on the level of technical and non-technical library personnel. They include the ability to:

- engage in sustained reasoning;

- manage complexity;

- test a solution;

- organise and navigate information structures and evaluate information;

- collaborate;

- communicate to other audiences;

- expect the unexpected;

- anticipate changing technologies;

- think about information technology abstractly.

Perhaps the last competency is the most essential. Thinking about information technology abstractly means reflecting on one's use of information technology and identifying 'commonalities that cut across technological experiences'. In the digital library environment, this could involve observing how information is organised and managed on commercial websites and asking, 'How can I apply this within my library setting?'

The report also advocates an understanding of information technology concepts including digital representation of information, information organisation, and algorithmic thinking and programming. A grasp of algorithmic thinking and programming among library staff charged with managing data in a digital library can be an enormous boon to efficiency. A cataloguer who designs their own scripts to update records in the library's ILS database can maintain that database much more effectively than one who is limited to editing functions prepackaged in an ILS.

How can library leaders move their staff in this direction? Training is one answer. Examples of libraries that have implemented training programmes for skills in specific technologies abound (Cuddy, 2002). More often than not, technology training initiatives focus on specific technological skills rather than broader competencies that enable people to develop creative technological solutions to problems. However, a recent article describes conceptual training in information technology at Georgian Court University library.

The trainer, a systems administrator and database administrator turned technology librarian, realised, as she was helping people with technical problems, that many lacked a basic understanding of fundamental technological concepts. She devised a training curriculum that covered basic computer and networking principles, as well as relational database design. The training challenged many employees, but the feedback that she received was largely positive. Only after this basic level of training did she introduce task-specific training (Waterhouse, 2005).

In general, managers can encourage creative thinking on digital library problems by challenging employees to come up with solutions rather than giving them highly prescriptive assignments. Managers must balance the need to standardise procedures and processes centrally with the flexibility needed to promote innovation by employees across the organisation.

As a library shifts towards developing a digital library, library management and staff need to adopt a more project-oriented perspective on work. Many aspects of traditional library work, such as cataloguing and reference, are based on routine operations. By contrast, most digital library work is project-based, whether it is the construction of a web portal or the implementation of a federated search system. Managers and team leaders should learn project management skills and employ project management software as they undertake digital library work. Even relatively small operations can benefit from small-scale project management strategies and lightweight project management software, which is now available as low-cost web applications.

Strategic planning

How should digital library work fit into the strategic planning of a library and its parent organisation? Rather than take a prescriptive approach to planning for a digital library, we will identify some crucial implications that digital library integration should have on any library strategic planning process.[4] These are:

- The organisational goals of a library and/or its parent organisation should drive digital library integration work.

- Possibilities that are created by digital technology can, in some cases, change the goals of an organisation, such as a university or public library.

- Because of the continuously evolving nature of the digital environment, libraries should not make detailed technological plans that look more than a few years ahead.

- Libraries need to position themselves to deal with change.

- The best way to influence the future course of digital libraries is to participate in community-wide efforts to develop standards, resources and services for the library community as a whole.

- Libraries should look to peer organisations as reference points when doing digital library planning.

- Libraries should look to developments in society in general as they plan for their digital library.

Fundamentally, the organisational goals of a library and its parent organisation should drive digital library goals. The decision to create a digital collections system, invest in federated searching software or customise a library web portal should all be driven by wider institutional objectives rather than simply following technology trends. Library leaders and technologists need to ask themselves, 'What is my institution about and where does digital library work fit in?'

At a public library, the focus might be on developing customised services for various groups of patrons, such as children, young adults or genre fiction readers. At a community college or urban university, the goal of digital library integration work might be to create simplified access to library resources for students conducting much of their research from off campus. At a private liberal arts college with a focus on teaching, digital library work might focus on customised databases or digital collections systems that provide strong support for instruction. At a research institution, the focus might be on providing comprehensive access to primary and secondary research material for graduate students and research-oriented faculty, as well as developing local digital collections.

While digital library goals should be driven by institutional goals, we must remember that possibilities offered by digital technology can, at times, change departmental and even institutional goals. For example:

- The Internet has enabled distance learning to become a high priority for some educational institutions at which it barely existed before.

- In many academic libraries, the delivery of information digitally has created an organisational goal of integrating library services and academic technology services.

- Most public libraries now consider the provision of Internet-connected computers to the public a fundamental part of their mission.

- The availability of archived journal content has caused some libraries to drop their goal of being a regional archive for that type of content.

- More streamlined interlibrary loan technology and online content now allow smaller academic libraries to consider support for faculty research an important and achievable aspect of their mission.

Because of the constant state of change in digital technologies, library leaders should focus on positioning their organisations for change. A single library, even a large one, is simply a minor actor in a digital world that is in constant flux. No matter how much foresight any library, large or small, has, there is no way that its planners can determine what its digital presence will look like in ten years.

As library leaders plan for digital initiatives, they should keep in mind that they are part of a broader digital library community that has produced some very innovative work. Successful standards, such as Dublin Core and the OpenURL, as well as open source software projects, such as DSpace and Fedora, have been driven by library involvement. Perhaps the greatest influence that libraries can have on their digital future is participation in initiatives that aim to develop new standards, technologies and services for the broader community.

Libraries share the same problems with other libraries of similar size and mission. Because of this, it is very easy for library leaders to use other libraries of their type as their sole reference point when planning and assessing their performance. Certainly, digital library planners should communicate and cooperate with libraries that are similar in mission and/or geographically close. However, to best fulfil their particular organisational mission, they should not be content to simply replicate the activities of peer organisations.

To solve digital library problems, library leaders must look outside the library world. New technologies that affect digital library development often emerge in the commercial world. Library leaders need to keep an eye on trends in electronic commerce, Internet search engines, online media delivery and consumer electronics. The world of academic information technology is particularly important for academic digital libraries, as there are often opportunities for integration and synergy between instructional technologies and digital libraries.

The future of digital library integration

While it is impossible to predict the digital library integration challenges that lie ahead, we can speculate about the future. We believe that five major factors will drive developments in digital library integration over the next five to ten years:

- more digitised content;

- greater aggregation of metadata and content;

- better systems for searching and discovery of content;

- an increasingly participatory role of the information seeker in digital library systems;

- better interoperability of digital library systems.

Driving all of these phenomena will be generally higher expectations for the way that information systems perform. These expectations will come from developments and trends in the wider world of web technology. At present, several leading trends in web technology have been corralled together under the mantra of Web 2.0. Generally speaking, these ideas point to a Web that is more interconnected and participative, both on the level of the software and databases that drive it as well as the human beings using it.

It is easy to predict that more content will become digital over the next ten years – but which content and to what effect on digital libraries? The existing trends of digitisation in serials publications, reference materials and special collections and archives should continue. The digitisation of monographic works, which has been underway for at least as long as the 35-year-old Project Gutenberg, appears to be gaining momentum in 2006. Google has announced plans to massively digitise the contents of major research libraries, while Amazon has announced plans to cooperate with publishers to sell electronic versions of books. The Open Content Alliance plans to make available as many public domain works as possible. By 2010 there will no doubt be a large corpus of public domain monographic works available on the Internet. And there will be new economic models in place for purchasing electronic books. Libraries might very well begin with acquiring the electronic rights to books that they purchase in print, and, as patrons become more comfortable with books in the electronic format, move to purchase electronic-only books.

In the current information landscape, libraries manage electronic content from many different publishers and information providers. That content is delivered using many different technologies. We believe that the economy of the information world will stay diversified, economically and technologically. Libraries will still need to manage accounts and subscriptions with many different information providers. Information will continue to arrive in many different formats, both physical and electronic. Electronic resource management systems that manage URLs, licence agreements, administrative information, etc., will continue to evolve and become an increasingly important part of a typical academic or public library's workflow.

There will, however, be changes to the sheer amount of high-quality information to which a library is able to provide access. Before the Internet economy, only a select group of books and music was available to the public due to the limited amount of inventory that a typical book or record store could carry. The 'long tail' phenomenon enabled by Internet businesses, such as Amazon now allows a huge number of what would once have been obscure books, music and videos (as well as other products) to survive and even flourish. Applying this logic to libraries, the amount of content provided by a library digitally should not be limited by the size of its physical 'store'.

Already, we might observe that relatively small public and academic libraries can, with the use of one general purpose full-text periodical index, provide their patrons with a much deeper collection of periodical literature than they could in their physical libraries before the Web. Small libraries, provided they have strong per-capita funding, should be able to provide their patrons with an increasing amount of information via their digital presence.

Libraries will still have to focus their purchases on content that fits their mission. But the difference in the amount of information available to a patron of a small college library focused on arts and humanities, and a large library also focused on arts and humanities will diminish. Both libraries will have access to the full corpus of secondary literature in the fields that they support. Quick-turnaround interlibrary loan systems for books and electronic article delivery for journal articles has already brought many academic libraries close to this reality. More aggregated packages of digital information in the form of electronic journals and books will expand the phenomenon. A library's funding will still determine the scope and quality of information that it can provide; however, per-capita funding will soon be better than absolute funding as an indicator of what the library can provide its patrons.

Libraries of the future will have more competition from other sources of information available on the Internet. Already, libraries must compete against online bookstores and a vast amount of information available openly on the Internet. Soon there may be commercial digital libraries that aggregate demand for the kind of information that public or academic libraries provide. Potential library patrons might decide that they would rather pay a fee for a superior commercial digital library than use the academic or public library with whom they are affiliated. Public and academic libraries will need to tailor their services to the communities that they serve in order to stay relevant.

Special collections and institutional repositories will be one important way that libraries stay relevant to their clientele and distinguish themselves from one another. These are collections that are of unique value to the library's own community or a special community of users. In the case of an academic library, they might include a special archive of primary materials as well as unpublished scholarly papers, research data and teaching materials. In the case of a public library, they might well be a digital photo archive or an index of a local newspaper. Attention to these types of collections will increase as what is now viewed as a library's main collection (published books, journal articles, etc.) is increasingly seen as a standard commodity available at many libraries of a given type and/or via other means on the Internet.

A single search box that searches all of a library's content, returning results in perfect order of relevance has been an elusive goal of digital library integration for some time now. In many ways, society's experience with Internet search engines has defined this goal. Digital library integrators are likely to be working hard over the next few years to achieve it using the awkward approach of federated searching. As discussed in Chapter 8, an alternative approach to federated searching is to harvest data from a variety of sources and put it in a single index that can be searched with a search engine.

Searching with a single search box is but one information discovery strategy that digital libraries will borrow from the wider Internet world. Digital libraries will need technologies that intelligently organise and link together the information they provide. Amazon provides a single search box, but it also provides many other ways of discovering relevant material, including recommendations for related items, links to works cited, consumer contributed reviews, etc. Digital libraries will develop their own means of providing linkages between intellectual works. For example, the California Digital Library has designed a system that uses historical circulation data to recommend related materials to library patrons (Whitney, 2006).

In many ways, integrated library systems still cling to the basic paradigm of the card catalogue. Records for books are downloaded from a bibliographic utility much as catalogue cards were printed out once a book was acquired. Once those records are downloaded to the system, they remain largely unchanged, even if the record is improved at the level of the bibliographic utility. When we search our web OPACs we search this static database. Digital libraries need to provide their patrons with dynamic databases that are continually updated and improved, and leverage the wealth of related content available on the Web. Eventually, searching a library catalogue should mean searching a subset of a database that is being continuously improved by the whole library community, if not the whole web community.

Improvements in information discovery strategies may also take the form of building specialised search engines tailored to a particular research need. Amazon recently introduced a service called Alexa, which allows independent programmers to create narrowly focused search engines using its giant search engine database. Besides creating repositories of specialised digital information, a new role for digital libraries might very well be building specialised search systems that interact with widely available data in new ways.

The digital library patron will play an increasingly participative role in the construction of digital libraries. A key Web 2.0 concept is that the collective intelligence of users should improve web applications. Library users will expect a social space in which they can participate in an interactive dialogue about the materials they find in the library. Already, public libraries are introducing online book clubs, and, in both academic and public libraries, library patrons are beginning to enrich online catalogues with online reviews.

In a certain sense, library patrons are already constructing their own mini digital libraries of content that that they collect and manage using social bookmarking software like del.icio.us and Connotea. Personal information management practices will have a tremendous impact on digital library design. Digital library integrators will need to pay attention to a wide range of online personal information management tools including newsreaders, citation management systems, research and writing tools, as well as other applications. Savvy library patrons may even take advantage of digital library web services' APIs to mash their own digital library applications. Digital library integrators will also need to pay attention to devices outside of the traditional PC that can be used to access and manage information. Patrons may very well want to download digital library content to their iPod, search research databases from their smart phone or read electronic reserve material on an e-book reader.

A key theme running throughout this book is that standards and interoperability are essential to creating successfully integrated digital libraries. If library software providers and content vendors adopt standards and APIs more broadly, digital library components will become more modular in the future. It will be easier to mix up digital library software components, metadata sources and content to form new applications with added value. Libraries will need to carefully choose standards that work with information sources inside and outside the library community.

Digital library integrators have an exciting future. The ever-changing digital information environment should continue to provide a continuous stream of integration challenges. Digital library integrators will turn these challenges into opportunities for creative solutions.

Summary

- Digital library integration work should occur throughout a library organisation, but technology specialists are also essential.

- A systems librarian or central systems office is the traditional model for providing across-the-board technical support in a library, including digital library integration work.

- Increasingly, libraries are dividing traditional systems or information technology work from digital library work.

- Public service librarians should help library patrons leverage the digital library through teaching and collaboration efforts; they should also help design, promote and evaluate digital library services.

- The mainstays of collection management work in the future will be electronic resource management and metadata creation for locally owned digital assets.

- Cross-functional teams can be useful for accomplishing digital library work that falls outside the formal organisational structure of a library, but sometimes libraries need to adjust their formal organisational structure to the operational requirements of running a digital library.

- Effective digital library integrators may or may not have formal training in library and information science.

- Employees in all areas of library work should recognise the possibilities of technology and leverage it to make their work more efficient.

- Information technology fluency among employees is essential for an organisation to leverage information technology; information technology fluency involves a more abstract level of understanding of information technology than skills-based technology training often provides.

- Managers should encourage information technology fluency through educational and training opportunities, and by challenging employees with projects that demand abstract thinking about technological problems.

- Much digital library integration work is project-based; library employees working on digital integration projects should become familiar with project management techniques.

- When planning for the future, libraries should consider the important implications of their digital presence.

- The future of digital library integration will include more digitised content, greater aggregation of metadata and content, better systems for searching and discovery of content, an increasingly participatory role for the information seeker, and better interoperability of information systems.

Notes

1 For an overview of the profession of systems librarianship see Wilson (1998).
2 Association of College and Research Libraries (2000) and Donham (2004) discuss aspects of information literacy and faculty librarian collaboration at academic libraries.
3 See: *http://www.washington.edu/students/crscat/lis.html* (accessed: 28 December 2005).
4 For a book that offers a prescriptive approach to technology planning in libraries see Matthews (2004).

Glossary: acronyms used in this book

AACR – Anglo American Cataloguing Rules
Ajax – Asynchronous JavaScript And XML
API – application programming interface
CD – compact disc
CGI – common gateway interface
CMS – content management system
COinS – context objects in spans
CSS – cascading style sheets
CSV – comma separated values
DAM – digital asset management
DHCP – Dynamic Host Configuration Protocol
DNS – domain name service
DOI – digital object identifier
DVD – digital versatile disc
EAD – Encoded Archival Description
EDI – electronic data interchange
EDIFACT – Electronic Data Interchange for Administration, Commerce, and Transport
EMRI – Electronic Resource Management Initiative
ERM – electronic resources management
ERMS – electronic resource management systems
FTP – File Transfer Protocol
HTML – HyperText Markup Language
HTTP – HyperText Transfer Protocol
ILL – interlibrary loan
ILS – integrated library system
IM – instant messaging
ISBN – International Standard Book Number
ISSN – International Standard Serial Number
IT – information technology

JISC – Joint Information Systems Committee
JPEG – Joint Photographic Experts Group
LAN – local area network
LDAP – Lightweight Directory Access Protocol
MARC – MAchine Readable Cataloging
METS – Metadata Encoding and Transmission Standard
MODS – Metadata Object Description Schema
MVC – model view controller
NCIP – NISO Circulation Interchange Protocol
NISO – National Information Standards Organization
NOS – network operating system
OAI – Open Archives Initiative
OAIS – Open Archival Information System
ONIX – ONline Information exchange
OPAC – Online Public Access Catalog
OSI – Open Systems Interconnectivity
OWL – Web Ontology Language
PAMS – publication access management service
PDF – Portable Document Format
PEAR – PHP Extension and Application Repository
Perl – Practical Extraction and Reporting Language
PHP – PHP Hypertext Preprocessor
PMH – Protocol for Metadata Harvesting
RADIUS – Remote Authentication Dial In User Service
RDBMS – relational database management system
RDF – resource description framework
REL – Rights Expression Language
RSS – really simple syndication
SICI – serial item and contribution identifier
SIP – Standard Interface Protocol
SOAP – Simple Object Access Protocol
SQL – Structured Query Language
SRU – search retrieve via URL
SRU/W – search/retrieve via URL or web service
SRW – search/retrieve via web service
SSL – secure sockets layer
SSO – single sign on
SUSHI – Standardized Usage Statistics Harvesting Initiative
TCP/IP – Transport Control Protocol/Internet Protocol
TEI – Text Encoding Initiative
TIFF – Tagged Image File Format

UPC – universal product code
URL – uniform resource locator
WYSIWYG – what you see is what you get
XHTML – eXtensible HyperText Markup Language
XML – eXtensible Markup Language
XSLT – eXtensible Stylesheet Language Transformations
XSS – cross site scripting

Bibliography

Allard, E. and Bisson, C. (2004) 'Portal integration: III and Campus Pipeline'; available at: *http://www.acrlnec.org/sigs/itig/IntegratingLibraryPortal.pdf* (accessed: 10 August 2005).

Anceson, C. (2004) 'The long tail', *Wired Magazine*, 12(10); available at: *http://www.wired.com/wired/archive/12.10/tail.html* (accessed: 22 December 2005).

Anon (2005) 'Mashing the Web'. *Economist* 376(8444) (Special Section): 4–6.

Association of College and Research Libraries (2000) *The Collaborative Imperative: Librarians and Faculty Working Together in the Information Universe*. Chicago: ACRL.

Berners-Lee, T., Hendler, J. and Lassila, O. (2001) 'The Semantic Web'. *Scientific American* 284(5): 34–44.

Breeding, M. (2005) 'Dynix announces Corinthian ILS for academic libraries'; available at: *http://www.librarytechnology.org/fulldisplay.pl?SID=2005080393078613&UID=&RC=11386&code=BIB&Row=12* (accessed: 9 August 2005).

Borgman, C. L. (1997) 'From acting locally to thinking globally: a brief history of library automation', *Library Quarterly* 67(3): 215–49.

Budapest Open Access Initiative (2002) 'Budapest Open Access Initiative'; available at: *http://www.soros.org/openaccess/read.shtml* (accessed: 25 January 2006).

Calhoun, L. (2005) 'Making PHP work for you: generating real time, customised Oracle reports for the Web'. Unpublished paper.

Campbell, J. D. (2006) 'Changing a cultural icon: the academic library as a virtual destination', *EDUCAUSE Review* 41(1): 16–31.

Carr, N. G. (2004) *Does IT Matter? Information Technology and the Corrosion of Competitive Advantage*. Boston: Harvard Business School Press.

Cervone, F. (2005) 'What we've learned from doing usability testing on OpenURL resolvers and federated search engines', *Computers in Libraries* 25(9): 10–14.

Collins, M. (2005) 'Electronic resource management systems: understanding the players and how to make the right choice for your library', *Serials Review* 31: 125–40.

Committee for Space Data Systems (2002) 'Reference model for an Open Archival Information System (OAIS)', *Blue Book* 1; available at: *http://ssdoo.gsfc.nasa.gov/nost/wwwclassic/documents/pdf/CCSDS-650.0-B-1.pdf* (accessed: 18 February 2006).

Cuddy, C. (2002) 'Designing a library staff computer training program: implementation of core competencies', *Information Technology and Libraries* 21(2): 87–90.

Dahl, M. (2004) 'Building an OpenURL resolver in your own workshop', *Computers in Libraries* 24(2): 6–8, 53–4, 56.

Davis, S. (2005) 'Electronic resources management from the field', *Serials Review* 32(2): 174–5.

De Rosa, C. (2005) *Perceptions of Libraries and Information Resources. Part 1: Libraries and Information Sources – Use, Familiarity and Favourability.* Dublin, Ohio: OCLC; available at: *http://www.oclc.org/reports/2005perceptions.htm* (accessed: 19 February 2006).

Dempsey, L. (2003) 'The recombinant library: portals and people'. Published simultaneously in *Journal of Library Administration* 39(4); and in Sul H. Lee (ed.) *Improved Access to Information: Portals, Content Selection and Digital Information.* Binghamton, NY: Haworth; pp. 103–36. Available online at: *http://www.oclc.org/research/staff/dempsey/recombinant_library/* (accessed: 23 February 2006).

Dempsey, L. (2005) 'The integrated library system that isn't'; available at: *http://orWeblog.oclc.org/archives/000585.html* (accessed: 5 August 2005).

Dempsey, L., Childress, E., Godby, C. J., Hickey, T. B., Houghton, A., Vinze-Goetz D. and Young, J. (2005) 'Metadata switch: thinking about some metadata management and knowledge organisation issues in the changing research and learning landscape', in D. Shapiro (ed.) *LITA Guide to E-Scholarship.* Available online at: *http://www.oclc.org/research/publications/archive/2004/dempsey-mslitaguide.pdf* (accessed: 15 January 2006).

Donham, J. (2004) 'Developing a culture of collaboration: librarian as consultant', *The Journal of Academic Librarianship* 30(4): 314–21.

Duke University Libraries (2003) 'Integrated Library System Advisory Group decision issues'; available at: *http://www.lib.duke.edu/its/diglib/ilstrans/selection/ILS_Decision_Issues.pdf* (accessed: 15 August 2005).

Evergreen Development Team (2006) 'Evergreen', Keynote speech presented at Code4lib Conference, Corvallis, Oregon, 14 February.

Fedora Development Team (2005) *White Paper*; available at: *http://www.fedora.info/documents/WhitePaper/FedoraWhitePaper.pdf* (accessed: 26 January 2006).

Ferguson, C. L. (2004) 'October: OpenURL link resolvers', *Computers in Libraries* 24(9): 17–24.

Fons, T., Reynolds, R. R. and Duncan, J. (2005) 'Serials standards: envisioning a solution to the online serials management mess', *Serials Librarian* 48(3/4): 302–14.

Foster, N. F. and Gibbons, S. (2005) 'Understanding faculty to improve content recruitment for institutional repositories', *D-Lib Magazine*, 11(1); available at: *http://www.dlib.org/dlib/january05/foster/01foster.html* (accessed: 14 February 2006).

Gardner S. and Eng, S. (2005) 'Gaga over Google? Scholar in the social sciences', *Library Hi-Tech* 22(8): 42–5.

Gibson Research Corporation (2005) 'The Gibson Research Corporation denial of service pages'; available at: *http://grc.com/dos/* (accessed: 17 February 2006).

Grogg, J. E. (2005) 'OpenURL linking with Google Scholar', *Searcher* 13(9): 39–46.

Hellman, E. (2005) 'OpenURL CoinS: a convention to embed bibliographic metadata in HTML'; available at: *http://ocoins.info/* (accessed: 12 January 2006).

Hendricks, A. (2003) 'The development of the NISO Committee AX's OpenURL Standard', *Information Technology and Libraries* 22(3): 129–33.

Herold, K. (2004) 'Customizing patron functions in web voyage and beyond'. Presentation given at the Endeavor Mid-Atlantic User's Group Meeting, April 2005, Syracuse, New York.

Hibbs, C. (2005) 'Rolling with Ruby on Rails'; available at: *http://www.onlamp.com/pub/a/onlamp/2005/01/20/rails.html?page=1* (accessed: 7 January 2006).

Higa, M. L. (2005) 'Redesigning a library's organisational structure', *College & Research Libraries* 66(1): 41–58.

Highsmith, A. (2002) 'MARC it your way: MARC.Pm', *Information Technology and Libraries* 21(1): 19–25.

Innovative Interfaces, Inc. (2005) 'Innovative announces three campus computing solutions'; available at: *http://www.iii.com/news/pr_template.php?id=255* (accessed: 10 August 2005).

Jacsó, P. (2004) 'Peter's Digital Reference Shelf', June; available at: *http://www.gale.com/servlet/HTMLFileServlet?imprint=9999&region=*

7&fileName=reference/archive/200406/crossref.html#img36 (accessed: 15 January 2006).

Jantz, R. and Giarlo, M. J. (2005) 'Architecture and technology for trusted digital repositories', *D-Lib Magazine* 1(6): doi:10.1045/june2005-jantz (accessed: 28 January 2006).

Jewell, T. and Pesch, O. (2006) 'SUSHI: Standardised Usage Statistics Harvesting Initiative'; available at: *http://www.ala.org/ala/lita/litamembership/litaigs/igstandards/SUSHI.pdf* (accessed: 8 February 2006).

Jewell, T. D., Anderson, I., Chandler, A., Farb, S. E., Parker, K., Riggio, A. and Robertson, N. D. M. (2004) 'Electronic resource management. The report of the DLF Initiative'. Digital Library Federation; available at: *http://www.diglib.org/pubs/dlfermi0408/* (accessed: 29 June 2005).

Jones, E. (2002) 'The exchange of serials subscription information', NISO White Paper; available at: *http://www.niso.org/Serials-WP.pdf* (accessed: 10 February 2006).

Kam-min, K. and Palmer, D. (2004) 'Upstream content management in an ILS. Downstream integrated access, authentication, portals & statistics'; available at: *http://www.ala.org/ala/lita/litaevents/2004Forum/CS_Upstream_Content_Mgmt.pdf* (accessed: 12 August 2005).

Lagoze, C., Payette, S., Shin, E. and Wilper, C. (2005) 'Fedora: An architecture for complex objects and their relationships', *International Journal of Digital Libraries*, doi: 10.1007/s00799-005-0130-3; draft available at: *http://www.arxiv.org/abs/cs.DL/0501012* (accessed: 14 February 2006).

Library & Information Statistics Unit (2004) 'LibPortal Project: a survey and review of library-oriented portals in higher and further education', Loughborough University.

Loussau, N. (2004) 'Search engine technology and digital libraries', *D-Lib Magazine* 10(6); available at: *http://www.dlib.org//dlib/june04/lossau/06lossau.html* (accessed: February 19 2006).

Malhotra, A. (2005) 'Seattle Public Library deploys RSS-based applications', *therssweblog*; available at: *http://rss.weblogsinc.com/2005/06/22/seattle-public-library-deploys-rss-based-applications/* (accessed: 24 March 2006).

Matthews, J. (2004) *Technology Planning: Preparing and Updating a Library Technology Plan.* Westport, CT: Libraries Unlimited.

Mazzocchi, S., Garland, S. and Lee, R. (2005) 'SIMILE: practical metadata for the Semantic Web', 26 January; available at: *http://www.xml.com/pub/a/2005/01/26/simile.html* (accessed: 24 February 2006).

National Research Council (1999) *Being Fluent with Information Technology*. Washington, DC: National Academy Press.

NISO (2005) 'ANSI/NISO Z39.88-2004. The OpenURL framework for context-sensitive services'; available at: *http://www.niso.org/standards/standard_detail.cfm?std_id=783* (accessed: 11 January 2006).

NISO SUSHI Working Group (2005) 'Standardized Usage Statistics Harvesting Initiative (SUSHI)': *http://www.library.cornell.edu/cts/elicensestudy/ermi2/sushi/* (accessed: 17 February 2006).

North Carolina State University Libraries (2006) 'NCSU Libraries unveils revolutionary, Endeca-powered online catalogue'; available at: *http://www.lib.ncsu.edu/news/libraries.php?p=1998&more=1* (accessed: 19 January 2006).

Northwestern University Library (2002) 'The cataloger's toolkit for Vger'; available at: *http://www.library.northwestern.edu/ctkv/#options_13* (accessed: 10 August 2005).

OCLC (year unknown) 'How the Open WorldCat program works'; available at: *http://www.oclc.org/worldcat/open/how/default.htm* (accessed: 8 August 2005).

OCLC (2005) 'Data dictionary for preservation metadata: final report of the PREMIS Working Group'; available at: *http://www.oclc.org/research/projects/pmwg/premis-final.pdf* (accessed: 14 February 2006).

O'Reilly, T. (2005) 'What is Web 2.0? Design patterns and business models for the next generation of software'; available at: *http://www.oreillynet.com/pub/a/oreilly/tim/news/2005/09/30/what-is-web-20.html* (accessed: 28 February 2006).

Pace, A. K. (2004) 'Dismantling integrated library systems', *Library Journal* 129(2): 34–6.

Pace, A. K. (2005) 'My kingdom for an OPAC', *American Libraries* 36(2): 48–9.

Peters, T. A. (2002) 'Digital repositories: individual, discipline-based, institutional, consortial or national?' *Journal of Academic Librarianship* 28(6): 414–17.

Price, G. (2004) 'Google partners with Harvard, Oxford & others to digitize libraries'; available at: *http://searchenginewatch.com/searchday/article.php/3447411* (accessed: 15 January 2006).

Price, G. (2005) 'A new digital library alliance makes its debut'; available at: *http://searchenginewatch.com/searchday/article.php/3553086* (accessed: 15 January 2006).

Reese, T. (2004) 'Information professionals stay free in the MARCEdit Metadata Suite', *Computers in Libraries* 24(8), 24–8.

Research Libraries Group (2003) 'Preserving our digital heritage', *RLG News* 56 (Spring); available at: *http://www.rlg.org/en/pdfs/rlgnews/news56.pdf* (accessed: 22 December 2005).

Rhyno, A. (2003a) 'From library systems to mainstream software: how web technologies are changing the role of the systems librarian', *Library Hi Tech* 21(3): 289–96.

Rhyno, A. (2003b) 'Dis-integrating ILSes'; available at: *http://sourceforge.net/mailarchive/message.php?msg_id=5010419* (accessed: 5 August 2005).

Sadeh, T. and Ellingsen, M. (2005) 'Electronic resource management systems: the need and the realisation', *New Library World* 106(5/6): 208–18; available at: *http://www.exlibrisgroup.com/resources/Electronic%20Resource%20Management%20Systems.pdf* (accessed: 24 March 2006).

Sirsi Corporation (year unknown) 'Sirsi Enterprise Portal Solution Featuring Rooms 2.0'; available at: *http://www.sirsi.com/Solutions/Prodserv/Products/eps.html* (accessed: 18 February 2006).

SGML Users Group (1990) 'A brief history on the development of SGML'; available at: *http://www.sgmlsource.com/history/sgmlhist.htm* (accessed: 17 February 2006).

Summann, F. (2004) 'Search engine technology and digital libraries: moving from theory to practice', *D-Lib Magazine* 10(9); available at: *http://www.dlib.org/dlib/september04/lossau/09lossau.html* (accessed: 19 February 2006).

Summers, E. (year unknown) 'MARC/PERL: MAchine Readable Cataloguing + PERL': *http://marcpm.sourceforge.net/* (accessed: 17 February 2006).

Tennant, R. (2004) *Managing the Digital Library.* New York: Reed Press.

University of California Libraries Bibliographic Services Task Force (2005) 'Rethinking how we provide bibliographic services for the University of California', The University of California Libraries; available at: *http://libraries.universityofcalifornia.edu/sopag/BSTF/Final.pdf* (accessed: 19 February 2006).

van de Sompel, H. (2001) 'Open linking in the scholarly information environment using the OpenURL framework', *D-Lib Magazine* 7(3); available at: *http://www.dlib.org/dlib/march01/vandesompel/03vandesompel.html* (accessed: 24 March 2006).

van Westrienen, G. and Lynch, C. (2005) 'Academic institutional repositories: deployment in 13 nations as of mid 2005', *D-Lib Magazine*, 11(9), doi:10.1045/september2005-westrienen.

Veblen, T. (1914) *The Instinct of Workmanship and the State of the Industrial Arts*. New York, NY: Macmillan.

W3 Consortium (1998) 'Extensible Markup Language (1.0)': *http://www.w3.org/TR/1998/REC-xml-19980210* (accessed: 17 February 2006).

Waterhouse, J. (2005) 'Technology training can be a piece of cake', *Computers in Libraries* 25(8): 16–18.

Waters, D. J. (2005) 'Managing digital assets in higher education: an overview of strategic issues', 28 October; available at: *http://www.arl.org/forum05/presentations/waters.pdf* (accessed: 24 March 2006).

Whitney, C. (2006) 'Generating recommendations in OPACS: initial results and open areas for exploration', code4lib Conference, 15–17 February, Corvallis, Oregon.

Wilson, T. C. (1998) *The Systems Librarian: Designing Roles, Defining Skills*. Chicago: American Library Association.

Yu, H. (2004) 'The impact of web search engines on subject searching in OPAC', *Information Technology and Libraries* 23(4): 168–80.

Zimmer, D. (2003) 'Real World XSS'; available at: *http://www.net-security.org/dl/articles/XSS-Paper.txt* (accessed: 17 February 2006).

Index

Printed in the United States
55080LVS00001BC/63

9 781843 341550